THE PRISCILLA PRINCIPLE

Making Your Life a Ministry

JO BERRY

 Zondervan Publishing House
Grand Rapids, Michigan

The Priscilla Principle: Making Your Life a Ministry
© 1984 by The Zondervan Corporation
1415 Lake Drive, S.E., Grand Rapids, Michigan 49506

Library of Congress Cataloging in Publication Data

Berry, Jo.
    The Priscilla principle.

    Bibliography: p.
    1. Christian life—1960–   . 2. Gifts, Spiritual.
3. Priscilla, Saint, 1st cent. I. Title.
BV4501.2.B417 1984   248.4   84-2188
ISBN 0-310-42631-6

Unless otherwise indicated, Scripture is quoted from the New American Standard Bible.

Edited by Evelyn Bence and Julie Ackerman Link
Designed by Ann Cherryman

Printed in the United States of America

84 85 86 87 88 89 89 / 10 9 8 7 6 5 4 3 2 1

THE PRISCILLA PRINCIPLE

Making Your Life a Ministry

DEDICATION

To George, for always pushing me toward God's will. And to my dear friend Jo Kreiger, who says she wants to be known for *not* writing a book, but whose words, thoughts, and ideas are so much a part of this one that I want to thank her for the way she has so consistently contributed to my spiritual growth and well-being over these many years.

Contents

Introduction

It was two weeks before the presidential elections, and automobiles everywhere were sporting bumper stickers lauding favorite candidates and espousing causes: *Yes* on 5; *No* on 15; Smith for senator; Rumpelstiltskin for representative. As I walked toward my car after my weekly Bible study, a woman near me stopped and read aloud the sticker on the bumper of a Cadillac. The owner of the car clearly supported a leading Democratic candidate for the presidency. "Wonder who that sticker belongs to?" she said. "And, I wonder what it's doing on a car that's parked at *this* church?"

Intrigued by her comments, I asked why she wondered what the car was doing in the church parking lot. "Because everyone knows that candidate is a liberal who favors abortion and the ERA. I can't believe anyone who would vote for him could be a Christian, so why would a supporter be at our church?"

Driving home, I started thinking about how ready and willing most of us are to label others, to impose on them our personal understanding and interpretation of terms, such as *liberal* or *conservative, mature* or *immature, godly* or *ungodly, right* or *wrong, Christian* or *unbeliever.* Our tendency to compartmentalize illustrates how much we Christians rely on labels and clichés and how misleading they can be.

For instance, most of us apply the term *Christian* to anyone who believes exactly as we do. I cannot count the number of prayer requests I've heard that started, "Please pray for so-and-so who is a Catholic and needs to know the Lord." Some such requests may be legitimate, but some of them embody the false assumption that Catholics are not Christians.

The term *full-time Christian service* is another misleading label. Actually, once a person accepts Jesus as Lord and Savior, he or she is engaged in full-time Christian service. There is no such thing as a part-time Christian. If we are called by the Father into membership in His family, every facet of our lives must be viewed as an ongoing ministry, dedicated to the Lord Jesus Christ.

Because of our own willingness to label, and because it is so convenient to do so, we misuse many critical terms. One word we commonly misapply is *ministry,* which may refer to anything from the office and duties of the pastor to changing diapers in the church nursery. Most Christians incorrectly equate it with church-based activities, yet both common sense and Scripture teach that ministry means much more than being involved in church work. In reality, once you become a Christian, your entire life is a ministry that relates to your roles, the places you live, work, and worship, and the people whose lives you touch. Somehow we've lost sight of that simple truth. Unfortunately, some Christians think of ministry more in terms of roles and duties within the church than as living a Christian lifestyle in an unbelieving world. As a result, they have developed church-centered, rather than Christ-centered ministries.

I fell into that trap myself. For several years my own misinterpretation of the word *ministry* severely limited my effectiveness and made me miserable. Oh, on the surface everything looked great. It appeared I had an active, successful ministry. I traveled around the country, speaking at retreats and seminars. I had made numerous tapes and written and published several Christian books, as well as magazine articles. I had even founded a center, dedicated to motivating women to minister effectively in their local churches. But something was missing.

Early in 1980 I stopped to reflect back, fifteen years before, when I had rededicated my life to Christ after having strayed for many years. I remembered how I hadn't been able to stop talking and thinking about Jesus; how I had been super-sensitive to the pain of others and how lost they were without Christ; how I hadn't been able to get enough of the Word. I had spent every spare moment devouring scripture, voraciously reading and studying the Bible. I had carried a New Testament with me wherever I went. I recalled how I had been consumed with the desire to saturate every area of my life with the presence of Christ. He'd been so real to me then. I thought about how I had sensed His presence every minute, about the precious, intimate times of prayer; at times I had literally heard His voice.

I wept, wondering what had happened to that Jo Berry. I had once loved to witness "cold turkey", and I had seized every opportunity—from striking up a conversation with the person behind me in the line at the grocery store to building on a casual hello to the mailman—to share the gospel. I still was spending time in the Word, although more out of duty than zeal, more to prepare myself for writing and teaching than because of my fervor. To an extent, my love for the Lord had diminished.

Furthermore, I realized that every area of my life revolved around Christians and the church. The bottom line showed that my ministry wasn't what it should, or could, be. I know now that by centering on the church, I had severely stunted my spiritual, intellectual, and emotional growth. I had confused serving the church with serving the Lord, and the two are not necessarily synonymous. There's a wide chasm between "churchianity" and active Christianity.

Beyond limiting my outreach, I had restricted my thoughts

and actions because I was letting my local church decide for me what my ministry should be. I had allowed it to dictate what I could or could not do, what I should or should not believe, and how I should interpret and apply Scripture, even when certain teachings conflicted with the leading of the Spirit in my life and with what I was convinced in my heart was true. Because I had abdicated the responsibility to work out my own salvation with fear and trembling, I was often trapped. Either I acted out of accord with those in authority in the church or I quenched the Spirit. No wonder I'd lost my joy and wasn't getting any satisfaction or pleasure from my ministry.

That day in 1980, as I cried and prayed, God showed me from His Word how I had erred. As I looked for comfort and answers, the Lord spoke directly to me from the pages of Scripture. He commended me for the good I had been doing in His name, but, at the same time, He warned me of a severe lack in my life. "'I know your deeds and your toil . . . and you have perseverance and have endured for My name's sake, and have not grown weary. But I have *this* against you, that you have left your first love'" (Rev. 2:2–4). I then realized what I had done: I had given pre-eminence to the church and delegated Christ to a secondary position.

I made a New Year's resolution that day. I vowed to renew my love relationship with my Lord, then to re-evaluate my present ministry and expand my vision. I wanted to bring balance and perspective back to my Christianity. I took what some people considered drastic measures, but for me they were necessary. I disbanded the center I had established. I resigned every position I held in the church. I stopped teaching my weekly Bible study. I canceled every speaking engagement on my calendar (some ran five years into the future—a bit presumptuous, don't you think?) and decided not to accept any more for at least a year. These changes were frightening to me, not only because I was giving up a sizable chunk of income but also because I'd been led to believe that if I weren't out and around my books wouldn't sell well. Even so, I determined to devote myself exclusively to writing and nurturing my relationship with my First Love—for the next twelve months.

The Lord has honored that decision in many ways. He and I are close again. During that year, I wrote *Beloved Unbeliever*, which became a bestseller. God has used it in magnificent ways and has blessed me in the process. I am once again accepting, and enjoy participating in, speaking engagements, but instead of automatically saying *yes* to the requests, (because I have a speaking ministry and feel it's required of me), I limit myself to a certain number of events each year, book no further than twelve months in advance, and carefully pray for and evaluate each opportunity God puts in my path. As a result, my speaking ministry is more fruitful. As for my fears about losing income, in 1980 God supernaturally led me to a major secular publisher who needed a freelance writer to develop Christian curriculum, and I am still employed part time by that firm. Most important, by forcing me to pull back and evaluate, the Lord showed me once again how to make my life a ministry. That's what this book is about.

ONE

The Meaning of Ministry

*"Now all these things are from God,
who reconciled us to Himself through
Christ, and gave us the ministry of
reconciliation"*
2 COR. 5:18.

A few months ago at a local seminary, I started a guest lecture about women and ministry by asking the students to share their definitions of *ministry*. None were the standard, cliché answers I had expected to hear. One young woman said ministry is serving God by serving others. Another replied that ministry is doing whatever God has called us to do. A young man noted that ministry is your life's work if you're planning to be a pastor.

"Only a pastor?" I asked. For several minutes we continued our discussion and the class concluded that ministry is the life work of every Christian. It isn't merely something we do or service to the church, but it involves living our faith, moment by moment, regardless of where we are or who we're with.

We don't have to look far into the pages of Scripture to validate that premise. Look at Jesus. He didn't hole up in the synagogues or hang out with religious leaders. The Gospels say He "went about." He ministered to people where they lived, whenever He saw needs. Look at Paul. He went to the people. He didn't care where or when he ministered, but wholeheartedly threw himself into doing what God had called him to, be it tentmaking or preaching.

Frequently, we think of Christ's last words as being the statements He made when hanging on the cross. Actually, His last spoken statement is recorded in Acts 1:8. What was on His heart right before His ascension? What was so relevant that He chose to embed it as a final charge in the minds of His followers? The last sentence Christ uttered was, "You shall receive power when the Holy Spirit has come upon you; and you shall be My witnesses both in Jerusalem, and in all Judea and Samaria, and even to the remotest part of the earth."

He spoke of His *provision* to us: the power He would bestow through the Holy Spirit. God supplies us with the strength, stamina, and ability to do whatever work He has ordained for us at any given moment. The presence of His Spirit within us helps us rise to the occasion. Because He is omnipotent, anything God asks us to do is reasonable from His point of view. Nothing is too hard or impossible for Him to accomplish. He is the dynamic of His own demands. When He told Moses to hold out his hand, the Red Sea parted. When He ordered Joshua's army to march around Jericho and blow their trumpets, the walls of the city fell outward. When He informed a bewildered Mary, through the angel Gabriel, that she was going to be the mother of the Messiah, He gave her the capacity to rejoice. When He called Saul, on the road to Damascus, to become an apostle, he was transformed. And when God calls us to minister, He provides a way for us to obey and gives us the power to perform.

Jesus also spoke of His *purpose* for us: "you shall be My witnesses." Shall be—a foregone conclusion. Christians are witnesses for Jesus Christ.

He also designated His *place* for us: in Jerusalem, Judea, Samaria, even to the remotest end of the earth. We start where we are—in our various Jerusalems—and move out, as He leads. In this last verbal directive, Jesus confirmed that every area of a disciple's life is to be a ministry.

Christ sends all believers, the universal church, into the world to minister for Him! In His great priestly prayer, shortly before He trod to Calvary, Jesus petitioned the Father on behalf of those who whould come after Him. He said, "I do not ask Thee to take them out of the world, but to keep them from the evil *one* . . . As Thou didst send Me into the world, I also have sent them into the world" (John 17:15, 18). That doesn't mean we are not supposed to serve in the local church, but it does mean we must not limit ourselves exclusively to that arena. We must view every aspect of life—home, school, marriage, family, community, neighborhood, place of employment, recreational facilities—as a potential place of service for the Lord Jesus.

The Purpose of Ministry

Accepting that any place is a place of ministry rejuvenates faith and revitalizes service. We no longer have to categorize certain things as being done "for the Lord" and other activities as being secular. Everything we do, from teaching a Bible lesson to grocery shopping, should be looked upon as a Christian ministry. But we aren't called to run around merely doing busy work for God. "God, . . . has saved us and called us with a holy life—not because of anything we have done, but because of His own purpose" (2 Tim. 1:8–9). There is a profound objective to our ministry: God's very own purpose, the same one that motivated the Father to send His Son to die for our sins. We have been called to *the ministry of reconciliation*: We minister so God can use us to bring others into a relationship with Jesus Christ.

Paul explained it this way: "God, who reconciled us to himself through Christ . . . gave us the ministry of reconciliation: that God was reconciling the world to himself in Christ, not counting men's sins against them. And he has committed to us the message of reconciliation" (2 Cor. 5:18–19). That message is salvation, the gospel, the good news that Jesus saves—that fallen, sinful, unregenerate humanity does not have to be permanently alienated from God.

The ministry of reconciliation is a restorative process. Many judicial systems have reconciliation courts where husbands and wives considering divorce come together and arbitrate their differences with a counselor, hoping that their relationship can be restored, or where members of families fractured by juvenile delinquency are brought together for help in sorting out their problems and for advice on how to heal the breach that has occurred. These courts try to restore families and marriages and to reconcile people who once had a love relationship but who have been alienated by the effects of sin.

Similarly, God uses Christians as counselors and advisors to help reconcile to Him people who have become His enemies as the result of sin. In the beginning, God created man and woman to have perfect fellowship with Him. Adam and Eve were immaculate in body and spirit; they were holy, totally without sin, and, therefore, were physically perfect, not subject to the aging process that culminates in death. They were created in the image of God and were like Him in every way but one: They had no knowledge of evil. Imagine! How blissful it must have been to be ignorant of sin. And, since Adam and Eve didn't know what sin was, they were incapable of transgressing. They would have remained in that perfect state, except. Except, they chose to eat from the one tree in the Garden that the Father, in love, had forbidden. They exercised their wills against God and, at the tempter's urging, sampled the fruit from the tree of the knowledge of good and evil, which opened their eyes to the meaning of sin. In a single act of disobedience Adam and Eve severed their love relationship with God, evoked His wrath, became His enemies, and passed on the knowledge of evil and the capacity for sin to all humankind. Since that fateful time, sin has been a never-ending source of hostility between God and humanity, whose disobedience set the creature at war against the Creator.

It's important to understand that when Adam and Eve broke faith, transmitting to all future generations their capacity to do evil, God didn't change. He did not become humanity's enemy, but He could no longer fellowship with us because God is holy and must remain separated from all that is evil. In His unending grace, God could not bear the hostility and separation between Him and those He created and loved. He yearned to restore men and women to their original position, to change them back from enemy to friend, so He sent Christ to be a peacemaker—to effect a reconciliation between Him and sinners.

Christ became the instrument of reconciliation between sinful man and woman and a holy God. His blood, shed on the cross, restores to the Edenic state those who apply it, in faith, to their lives. "For . . . while we were enemies, we were reconciled to God through the death of His Son" (Rom. 5:10). Once we are personally reconciled, we become ministers of reconciliation. God uses us to lead others back into a right relationship with Him.

We do this by showing others what Jesus is like and by telling them about Him. Example is the primary tool of reconciliation. We are "always carrying about in the body the dying of Jesus, that the life of Jesus also may be manifested in our body. For we who live are constantly being delivered over to death for Jesus' sake, that the life of Jesus also may be manifested in our mortal flesh" (2 Cor. 4:10–11). The word *manifest* means to be real enough, tangible enough, to hold in our hand. Through the way they live, Christians bring Jesus alive to others. When people have contact with those of us who are ministers of reconciliation, they should feel as if they are with Jesus. We speak to them as Christ would have spoken, touch them as He would have touched, love them as He loves. We also verbally tell others about Jesus. "We proclaim him, admonishing and teaching everyone with all wisdom, so that we may present everyone perfect in Christ" (Col. 1:28 NIV). But we must always remember that words without a valid example are empty and meaningless.

Paul viewed our role in the ministry of reconciliation as that of ambassadors for Christ. An ambassador is an official envoy of high rank who is a resident representative of his or her ruler. An ambassador is obligated to represent and uphold the interests and ideas of the party he or she represents and to negotiate a peaceful settlement during times of conflict. We are such envoys for the Ruler of the universe, the King of Kings, and Lord of Lords. As ambassadors for Christ we have been called, chosen, and sent by Him into the world to represent Him to those who do not know Him and to reconcile the differences created by sin.

Chosen and Appointed by God

We often think of the call to ministry as being issued exclusively to the clergy—to seminarians, pastors, or missionaries—but the Bible teaches that every Christian has been called into ministry by the Lord. One of the most passionate portions of Scripture is Jesus' talk with His disciples immediately before His death (John 13–17). He knew His time was short when He gave this final instruction. He wanted His followers to grasp the importance of their continuing role in the furtherance of the kingdom. In John 15:16 He explained to them their calling and responsibility. This passage also describes our responsibility as His disciples in this present age. "You did not choose Me, but I chose you, and appointed you, that you should go and bear fruit, and *that* your fruit should remain, that whatever you ask of the Father in My name, He may give to you" (John 15:16).

First, Christ clarified that He chose us to be His disciples. Being a disciple is not something we decide on our own to be; it is an act of sovereign, divine selection. That the Almighty hand-picked us, as incomplete and imperfect as we are, with all our spiritual chinks and fleshly vulnerabilities, is mind-blowing. We should be awed by such trust and responsibility. Being chosen by the Lord of the universe is a special privilege indeed.

Next, Jesus explained that we are not only chosen, but appointed. Just as the leader of a country appoints his ambassadors, Christ, the Head of the church, assigns each of us to a position in His kingdom. He has prepared something unique for each of us to do. He has put each of us where we are now, in the particular place we live and work, to minister to specific people for definite reasons. We are where we are now because Christ chose and ordained it to be so.

Christ said we are chosen to bear fruit. Fruitbearing involves many activities, from bringing souls into the family of God to being used to edify and uphold the saints. And the fruit we bear is a special kind: it is *remaining* fruit. It is imperishable; it never rots and can't be consumed. It propagates itself and has permanent, eternal value.

Let me share from my own life an example of *remaining* fruit. Many years ago, shortly after I rededicated my life to the Lord, I started talking about Jesus to my neighbor across the street. The change in me had been so drastic, she naturally wondered what had happened. She was especially impressed by how excited my family and I were about going to church and reading the Bible. She and her husband were religious and belonged to a church, but they attended sporadically and then only out of social obligation. They were good, moral people but they did not know the Lord.

She and I became close friends. We car-pooled the kids to school. I kept her company in the evenings when her husband worked the late shift. We went shopping, played Monopoly, baked cookies, and discussed Scripture—all the things that weave the fabric of friendship. I shared what God was doing in my life. After several months she asked if she could go to prayer meeting with us. I tried to act nonchalant and said, "Of course." Soon she was going to church with us on Sundays and taking her sons to Sunday school. Finally, she asked her husband to come with us. He claimed his negative response was out of loyalty to his own church, but his lack of interest was obvious.

My neighbor was terribly troubled by her husband's refusal and his coolness toward her renewed religious fervor. One night, after a family quarrel, she called and asked me to pray that God would make her husband want to go to church. "I want you to pray because I know your prayers get through," she said.

I assured her that hers would too—if she would make a personal commitment to the Lord, as I had. She asked me to come over and talk with her and within minutes she had prayed to receive Christ. Over the next few months her entire family accepted the Lord. Her husband became actively involved at the church and was elected to the position of trustee the following year.

Sadly, my friend and her husband divorced some years later, when their boys were going through the crucial stages of adolescence. It would have been easy for the boys to have walked away from the Lord. After all, it seemed their parents had. The children had been traumatized, their home disrupted, and they had been left pretty much to their own devices. The situation broke our hearts. George and I labored in prayer for all of them, especially the boys.

But this summer we had the privilege of attending the wedding of the oldest son. He has made a career in Christian music and married a delightful woman. His younger brother, a Marine, was his best man. He is happily married and the father of a darling baby girl. Both boys openly love the Lord and are establishing Christian families. Their father has remarried and seems happy, although he has nothing to do with the church. Their mother moved to New York State after the divorce and was so embittered she denied her faith for several years. Just a few months ago she let the Lord have His way in her life again.

On the way home from the wedding reception, George and I were talking about how proud we were of our "spiritual grandchildren" and how grateful we were for a second generation of fruit in our lives.

Living life as a ministry is like throwing a pebble into a pond. One tiny stone makes dozens of ripples and stirs up the entire body of water. "Our deeds are like stones cast into the pool of time. Though they themselves disappear, their ripples extend to eternity" (Anonymous). One small deed done, one person thoughtfully touched, one word spoken in concern can unknowingly touch dozens of lives. Seeds are tiny, but one small grain of corn will reproduce a stalk with ten or more ears and hundreds of seeds. You never know how much remaining fruit one little act will bear, how God will use one small good deed to turn someone's life around. A hand on a shoulder, an offer to pray for someone's child, a thank you when no one else remembered to say it—all are seeds of grace.

The Content of Ministry

A vital ministry involves four major components: Touching, telling, teaching, and toiling. *Touching* is first because it is foundational to all of the others. I am amazed at how often we talk about having a "personal" relationship with Jesus Christ, yet how impersonally we treat others, especially those who do not believe as we do. When the unemployed tell us they need food, we refer them to a social service agency or suggest they contact the deacon's fund. When a wife confides that she is having marriage problems, we recommend a marriage counselor at the church. When distraught parents weep over disobedient or straying children, we give them a how-to book or a set of teaching tapes. It seems that everything has been reduced to a formula and fit into a program. In trying to develop efficiency, we've lost the personal touch implied in the word *ministry*.

Touching means becoming involved with people in practical ways—giving of yourself and your substance—and it requires personal sacrifice. Writing a check or sending a sympathy card is easier and less emotionally demanding than taking someone shopping for groceries or paying a condolence call, casserole in hand. Touching takes time and effort but Christ taught, both by example and in the parables, that intimacy is an effective ministry's key ingredient. He went so far as to say that cup-of-water ministries are the criteria God uses to judge His own.

Jesus told of a judgment, when the sheep will be separated from the goats: "Then the King will say to those on His right, 'Come, you who are blessed of My Father, inherit the kingdom prepared for you from the foundation of the world. For I was hungry, and you gave Me *something* to eat; I was thirsty, and you gave Me drink; I was a stranger, and you invited Me in; naked, and you clothed Me; I was sick, and you visited

Me; I was in prison, and you came to Me.' Then the righteous will answer Him, saying, 'Lord, when did we see You hungry, and feed You, or thirsty, and give You drink? And when did we see You a stranger, and invite You in, or naked, and clothe You? And when did we see You sick, or in prison, and come to You?' And the King will answer and say to them, 'Truly I say to you, to the extent that you did it to one of these brothers of Mine, *even* the least *of them*, you did it to Me.'" (Matt. 25:34–40).

Note that the righteous sheep, who were helping others in practical ways, did not think of their everyday tasks as a service for the Lord. They made the same mistake as many of us; they did not view their every action as a ministry. Yet, the message is clear. Christ defined pure ministry as being your brother's keeper, as performing common (and what some people might consider inconsequential) acts, which contribute to the welfare and comfort of others—not only fellow-believers, but all people.

The deeds Christ mentioned as notable are not "religious" activities; they are life necessities: feeding the hungry, giving drink to the thirsty, being hospitable to strangers, clothing the naked, and visiting the sick and imprisoned. They are not showy acts; they won't bring acclaim or recognition, but they bring eventual eternal reward from the Lord. James, too, validated the premise that lovingly meeting basic, human needs is the essence of ministry. He wrote, "This is pure and undefiled religion in the sight of *our* god and Father, to visit orphans and widows in their distress, *and* to keep oneself unstained by the world" (James 1:27).

Emotional sensitivity is also a part of touching. Jesus was ultra-sensitive to the pain and needs of others. Many times He ministered to them without their asking. He insisted on feeding the huge crowd which had been following Him for many hours, before He taught them further. To provide food for their meal, He multiplied one boy's lunch of loaves and fishes.

The woman who had been hemorrhaging for twelve years merely touched the fringe of His garment and immediately was healed. When that happened, elbows were poking Jesus in the ribs and people were grasping at His hands and clutching at His arms, but He knew that one who had touched Him had a special need. When the woman realized the Lord was responding personally to her need, she fell down and worshiped Him. Her life was changed because He was sensitive to her desperation—even in the midst of a pushy crowd, even when He was in a hurry, even though He was on His way to something that seemed much more important than ministering to one isolated, ailing woman.

Our personal relationship with Christ must reflect in our personal relationships with others. We have to expose ourselves to their problems, hurts, pains, and joys. We must be willing to get involved with those whom God sets in our path.

Telling, or witnessing to others about the Lord, is also a component of ministry. We harbor many misconceptions about the meaning of witnessing. Most of us think of it as cornering somebody and sharing the steps of salvation. When the Spirit has prepared hearts, that method is valid and effective, but witnessing is far more than hitting someone over the head with your faith. The word *witness* takes its root from the word *martyr* and refers to one who testifies truly about what he or she has seen, heard, or knows to be true. Our role as witnesses for Christ is the same as that of a witness in court. All a courtroom witness is expected or allowed to do is tell what he or she knows from firsthand experience. It is not the duty of a witness to render a verdict, to convict the person or to pronounce sentence; those duties belong to the jury or judge. In the spiritual realm, conviction is the responsibility of the Holy Spirit. Christ explained it this way: "When the

Helper comes . . . He will bear witness of Me, and you *will* bear witness also" (John 15:26–27). It is not our job to convert or save people. Our witness springs from the moving of the Spirit in our lives and the end result belongs to God. We tell; the Spirit performs. We testify; He transforms. We are simply witnesses to the truth.

Ministry also includes *Teaching* about the Lord, both by word and deed. In each personal encounter, every Christian communicates something about his or her relationship with Christ. This relational teaching involves more than presenting facts from Scripture. Paul saw it as inscribing impressions of Christ into the hearts of others by the way we live. "You are a letter of Christ, cared for by us, written not with ink, but with the Spirit of the living God, not on tablets of stone, but on tablets of human hearts" (2 Cor. 3:3). Your life is a teaching tool by which others learn about Jesus. It is up to you whether it is a primer or an advanced course.

Christ commanded us, as His disciples, to teach others about Him. He said we should teach them "to observe all that I commanded you" (Matt. 28:20). The majority of this instruction is transmitted by showing rather than verbalizing. We teach others to love by being loving; we teach them fairness by treating them justly; we teach them how to cope with sorrow by grieving with them.

Unbelievers expect Christians to respond differently than other people. They may be ignorant about the spiritual things of God but they seem intrinsically to know that those who identify themselves with Jesus should handle life different from and better than those who do not. The world expects Christians to be pure—not to smoke, get drunk, or use foul language. Non-Christians expect Christians to be understanding, loving, trustworthy, fair, and to expend themselves for others. In short, the world expects Christians to be like Jesus, and, like it or not, they have a right to demand that of us. The apostle John noted that "the one who says he abides in Him ought himself to walk in the same manner as He walked" (1 John 2:6).

A word of caution. Don't deliberately try to set yourself apart by making an issue of your never taking a drink or never going to restricted movies or listening to rock music; you'll turn people off with your "holier than thou" attitude. Your actions will speak for themselves. The secret of reaching out into the world is to be *in* it without being *of* it. We must integrate into it without becoming attached to it, and we must heed John's warning: "Do not love the world, nor the things in the world" (1 John 2:15). Your disinterest and lack of intrigue with the things that attract unbelievers is a potent, silent witness.

A fourth aspect of ministry is *Toiling*. The word *toil* refers to the kind of hard labor that results in extreme weariness and sometimes in pain. I exercise regularly and when I get to the place where I can do my routine without "feeling" it, I know it's time to add more strenuous activities or to work out longer. The same is true of ministry. When we get to the place where we're comfortable with everything we're doing or if life is going too easily, it's time to stretch our faith muscles and toil.

Toiling means sacrificing time and material possessions and becoming emotionally vulnerable to others. Living a Christlike lifestyle takes effort and thought. Scripture frequently speaks of ministry being hard work! Several times Paul mentions laboring for the Lord. He said, "We toil, working with our hands" (1 Cor. 4:12). He commended the woman who shared his "struggle in the cause of the gospel" (Phil. 4:3). He praised a co-worker named Mary, who, he noted, "worked hard for you" (Rom. 16:6). And he complimented Persis, the beloved, who "worked hard in the Lord" (Rom. 16:12).

Although the work of life ministry isn't easy, it is always

productive. Our labor in the Lord is never wasted and is always noticed and somehow rewarded by Him. Paul exhorts us to "be steadfast, immovable, always abounding in the work of the Lord, knowing that your toil is not in vain" (1 Cor. 15:58). He encourages us to remain *steadfast*, which denotes a fixed position. Our eternal position is in Christ, and if we stand firm where He has put us and let nothing move us, He will stabilize us as we serve.

Paul then challenges us to be *immovable*. We must be unwavering in our faith and cling tenaciously to the One in whom we believe, never forgetting that whatever we do, we are doing for God's glory.

Finally, lest we slack off, Paul urges us to be *always a-bounding* in the work of the Lord. We are to overflow with good works, doing more than is expected or required of us and actually seeking ways to serve.

The first time I saw Niagara Falls, I thought about the "always abounding" part of this verse. As water, water, and more water kept spilling over in a never-ending flow, I realized that our service for the Lord should also be a ceaseless overflow—an overflow of works issuing from our faith. As we abound in the work of the Lord and are committed to the tasks He sets before us, we can rest assured that our toil is never in vain.

Everything we do in the Spirit counts for eternity.

TWO

Sacrificial Servants

*"Whoever wishes to become great
among you shall be your servant; and
whoever wishes to be first among you
shall be slave of all"*

MARK 10:43–44.

A few weeks ago I attended a meeting at the posh home of a wealthy woman. I'm afraid I didn't pay much attention to the planning session because I was so intrigued by the fact that she had a maid, complete with black uniform and white ruffled apron.

I know women who have cleaning ladies who come in once or twice a week, and several of my more fortunate friends have gardeners, but I'd never been in a home where the hostess had a full-time, live-in maid. I was struck by the differences the presence of a maid makes in a woman's life. The woman of the house never answers the door or the telephone. She doesn't clean her house or make her beds or do her own grocery shopping. When she wants a cup of tea she rings for the maid instead of going out to the kitchen and putting on the teakettle. Her servant is her hands and feet.

I was equally fascinated by the maid's performance. Regardless of what she was asked to do, she was immediately responsive to her mistress. She never balked about what she was asked to do or questioned why she was being told to do it. She simply responded, "Yes, ma'am," and obeyed.

As I was driving home, I started thinking about what being a servant means: total obedience, undivided loyalty, and immediate responsiveness to a master. As Christians we are called to be servants. We are Christ's hands; we are His feet. We owe Him total obedience, undivided loyalty, and immediate response. That simple truth is intrinsic in the teachings of Christ and lavishly evident in the early church. But today, power, title, and position, rather than servanthood, are emphasized in the Christian community. We don't talk much about sacrifices people make serving others; instead, we echo the names of Christian celebrities and prominent leaders more often than the name of Jesus. We quote from Christian books and sermon tapes as readily as from Scripture. Dr. Donn Moomaw has aptly observed that, "Faith in God has become more a public slogan than a private power." Somehow, we need to revive in our lives the biblical concept that service, not celebrity, is the essence of service.

The Lord presented a formula for achieving greatness in ministry. It is contrary to everything the world believes about gaining status and recognition. It doesn't make sense from a human standpoint, but it is God's way. Jesus said, "Whoever wishes to become great among you shall be your servant; and whoever wishes to be first among you shall be slave of all. For even the Son of Man did not come to be served, but to serve, and to give His life a ransom for many" (Mark 10:43–45). Four words stand out in those verses: servant, slave, serve, and give. Christians attain greatness through serving; they gain prominence and recognition by being slaves, not by telling others what to do or how they should believe or behave. And our service is to all people, not just to a select group. Reputation (greatness) comes from serving and we attain position (become first) when we stoop to serve. "Humility goes before honor" (Prov. 18:12). We get by giving, we succeed by serving.

In God's eyes, positions and titles do not matter. Jesus disregarded them. He was no respecter of persons. Mark 10 tells the story of His disciples trying for such power, but Jesus wouldn't hear of their talk; He told them of a new way, the lowly way of service.

Stooping to Serve

Jesus reinforced His teaching about serving when He washed His disciples' feet. He and the Twelve had just eaten what has come to be known as the Last Supper. Jesus was fully aware that Judas was going to betray Him and that His crucifixion was imminent. There were hundreds of things He could have said to His disciples at that time. He could have reminisced about the good times they had spent together, recalling the miracles, the close calls they'd had, the way the crowds had followed them everywhere. He could have reminded them of the time He had walked on the water, multiplied the loaves and fishes, or joked with them about the time they were frightened about being caught at sea in a storm. He could have read Scripture with them and had a prayer session. He could have gone to the temple and delivered one final, magnificent dissertation. But instead, after their last meal together, Jesus girded Himself with a towel, poured water into a basin, and began washing the disciples' feet. Probably a hush fell over the room as He stooped before them and tenderly touched their calloused skin. Scripture doesn't record how many pairs of feet the Lord bathed and dried before He got to Peter, but when He started to minister to Peter, he objected. "Lord, do you wash my feet?" (John 13:6).

Why did Peter ask such a question? Foot washing was a

common custom in biblical times. Occasionally a host, or a wife of the host, would wash the feet of a special guest but the job usually belonged to a bondservant. Obviously, Peter couldn't reconcile Christ's position as Lord with the service He was performing. He still did not comprehend that Jesus was both Lord and Servant. So, in his usual blustery, flamboyant fashion, Peter took it upon himself to tell Jesus what to do: "Never shall You wash my feet" (v. 8).

I don't think he meant to be rude or disobedient; he honestly believed that Jesus should not be washing his feet. He was his Lord! Peter thought Jesus should be catered to and served by the disciples; He was "better" than they and shouldn't lower Himself to the position of a slave.

When Peter rejected Christ's service, Jesus said, "If I do not wash you, you have no part with Me" (v. 8). That simple statement contains an amazing truth. Jesus Christ wants and needs to minister to us. Our relationship with Him cannot be a one-sided kinship where we serve Him but do not accept His service to us. How often we shut Him out, as Peter tried to do, by refusing His ministry in our lives. We try to do everything ourselves. We don't share our griefs, problems, joys, or triumphs with Jesus. We push Him away, hindering the development of intimacy. We must let the Lord impart Himself to us by receiving His service, then we, in turn, impart Him to others as we minister to them.

When the Lord finished washing the disciples' feet, He asked them if they understood what He had done for them. He wanted to make certain they had finally learned the meaning and importance of servanthood. He had repeatedly taught them about it, but the idea hadn't penetrated. Now, it had to. Time was running out.

When no one responded to His question, He explained His actions to them: "You call Me Teacher and Lord; and you are right, for *so* I am. If I then, the Lord and the Teacher, washed your feet, you also ought to wash one another's feet. For I gave you an example that you also should do as I did to you" (vv. 13–15). Christ verified that the disciples had not been mistaken about His high position. He was (and is) Lord God in the flesh, the Messiah, Savior. He was (and is) the great Teacher. But that did not negate the fact that He was also a servant.

His message to them and to us is that no person is ever too high in position or authority to perform lowly tasks. Jesus showed us the characteristics of a servant by His words and actions. He served in humility. He gave, sacrificing His life. We should serve in like manner. We must act on the truth of Jesus' words and example. Sacrificial service is the essence of ministry.

The Qualifications of Service

Along with being willing to serve and give, Jesus also taught that His followers must be willing to meet certain demands. Sacrifice involves giving our wills, our time, our possessions, our emotions, and sometimes our relationships. It may mean giving up easy-living for consecrated service. Immediately after Peter had testified that Jesus was the Christ the Son of the living God, the long-awaited Messiah, Jesus listed five qualifications for service—demands He makes on each of us. It was as if He had been thinking, "Okay, now that you know who I am, this is what you have to do about it." He told His disciples, "If anyone wishes to come after me, let him deny himself and take up his cross, and follow me" (Matt. 16:24).

This charge is an individual invitation, to each disciple separately to any*one*, not to a collective group. Despite the demand, Christ gives us a choice, so the first qualification for service is *wishing to serve*. The word *wish*, as used in that statement, means *to desire; to want to do something*. God is love and love never forces. True love respects and nurtures choice. So, becoming a dedicated servant starts with our personal desire to subject our wills to God's and sublimate ourselves to the position of a servant. We have to *want* to become Christ's servant before we can become one.

The second qualification for service is *coming after Christ*. He must be first, the number one priority in our lives, more important than anything or anybody. Our wills, wants, and comfort come after His. We give Him pre-eminence, put Him first in all things. When we put Him first, we acknowledge His Lordship. We are the servants, He is the Master.

The third qualification for service is *denying self*. Self-denial is not demeaning self or playing the martyr. It is relinquishing control of our lives to the Spirit. If there is a conflict between the flesh and the Spirit, we are to deny ourselves in lieu of God. It means obeying the Holy Spirit instead of following our natural instincts. Self-denial is submission in the purest sense: exercising the freedom not to insist on our own way in favor of doing God's will. It is what Christ exemplified when He knelt in the Garden of Gethsemane, knowing full well the cost of such obedience, and agonized, "Not as I will, but as Thou wilt" (Matt. 26:39).

The fourth qualification for service is *taking up your cross*. I have heard some of the most negative, heart-rending, sad, sorrowful interpretations of this phrase. Many Christians equate taking up their cross with spiritual drudgery and think it means that God will give them horrible problems to carry around so they can try to act happy in the midst of their trials. Nothing could be further from the truth. Our cross can't refer to burdens because the Lord has commanded us to yoke ourselves with Him and cast our cares on Him. Also, He's instructed us to bear one another's burdens, not our own. So the concept that our cross is some kind of spiritual oppression doesn't match up with the rest of Scripture.

Neither can taking up our cross mean we have to carry around the weight of our sin, because the guilt and shame of our sin was negated by Christ at Calvary. And taking up our cross can't mean that Christian service will be unpleasant, dreary, and burdensome or that God will call us to a task we absolutely abhor or aren't good at, because Christ promised us full joy.

Taking up our cross is doing the specific life ministry God has called us to do, those special things the Lord has prepared for each of us as individual disciples. It is carrying Christ's banner, which is the cross, into service. It is doing our part, just as Jesus did when He carried that rugged, splintered, heavy, back-breaking rood up the hill. Taking up your cross is picking up and performing your God-assigned tasks. Your cross is your ministry, and if you don't carry it, who will? If you don't take it up, it stays put.

The fifth qualification for service is *following Christ*, or trailing behind Him. We must not run ahead of God. We follow Jesus, not ourselves or someone else. He precedes us and we bring up the rear. Sheep follow the shepherd. When we follow in His footsteps, we acknowledge His leadership. We loyally serve and give wherever He leads.

The Rewards of Service

The demands of servanthood may seem stringent, but both the temporal and eternal rewards for service are lavish. Although we don't serve so we can receive rewards, we certainly should be motivated by the benefits that await us. One of the greatest rewards of serving comes from knowing that we are being used by the Lord. Nothing equals that sense of accomplishment. It comes in little, unexpected ways. I will never forget the time I was doing a seminar on self-esteem in Wichita, Kansas. A woman in her early twenties came up to me after one of the sessions and, with tears in her eyes, took my hand and said, "Do you have time for me to tell you a story?" I suggested we retreat to a pew on the platform so we could be alone.

She shared that one night, about a month before, she had been lying in bed seriously contemplating suicide. She had just broken up with her boyfriend, was having a severe disagreement with her parents, and multiple problems on her job. She was taking some classes at a local university and was flunking one of the courses she most needed. "I felt totally alone, like even God had deserted me. I thought, what have I got to live for? Nobody would care if I died."

As she reached for the container of pills on the night-stand, she noticed a copy of my book on self-image next to the lamp. A friend had given it to her the previous week but she had been in such a bitter, depressed mood that she hadn't wanted to read it. "On a whim," she explained, "I picked it up and started leafing through it. When I started reading I couldn't stop. It was like God was using your book to answer every question in my life."

When she looked directly at me and said, "I just wanted to tell you in person that you saved my life," I was so overwhelmed I started crying. When I wrote that book I never dreamed the Lord would use it to keep someone from killing herself. To think He did that with printed words on pieces of paper is mind-boggling. If that lovely young woman had been the only person who ever bought or read that book, all of the months of effort I put into it would have been worth it. What a beautiful, unexpected reward for my ministry.

We also receive eternal rewards for our service. The Bible teaches that "we must all appear before the judgment seat of Christ, that each one may be recompensed for his deeds in the body, according to what he has done, whether good or bad" (2 Cor. 5:10). Let me assure you, this is not a negative judgment! This is the judgment of believers by their Lord, for reward. It is not to decide whether or not we will receive eternal life and enter heaven because we already have eternal life in Christ. It is not so God can punish us for our sin because we are justified in Christ; He bore the penalty of our sin on the cross. It isn't for dealing with unconfessed sin because all of our sin, past, present, and future, was negated by Christ's death and resurrection. All who belong to Christ will appear and be compensated for their deeds. Any service we have performed as unto the Lord will be rewarded. Any deeds done that were not works of faith will be discarded. It's rather like going to court to receive a settlement after having won the case.

Christ, the Great Judge, will test the quality of all our deeds. "If any man builds upon the foundation with gold, silver, precious stones, wood, hay, straw, each man's work will become evident; for the day will show it, because it is to *be* revealed with fire; and the fire itself will test the quality of each man's work. If any man's work which he has built upon it remains, he shall receive a reward. If any man's work is burned up, he shall suffer loss; but he himself shall be saved, yet so as through fire" (1 Cor. 3:12–15).

The judgment of Christ is for reward, and no Christians need ever to fear losing their salvation. If that were possible, we would have to "work" our way to God, rather than accept Him through faith in Christ. Coming up empty-handed is the worst that can happen to us when we are judged.

Paul taught that this judgment is actually an opportunity for believers to make an accounting to the Lord, to present the ledger of our lives, the debits and credits being "Done in Christ" and "Done in Self." "For we shall all stand before the judgment seat of God . . . . So then each one of us shall give an account of himself to God" (Rom. 14:10, 12). We should be motivated to serve so that our ledgers end up "in the black."

Once our works have been tried by fire (1 Cor. 3:11–15), a

joyous celebration will begin. God will not condemn us for our failures; "there is no condemnation for those who are in Christ Jesus" (Rom. 8:1). Instead "then each man's praise will come to him from God" (1 Cor. 4:5).

Scripture lists five basic rewards, called crowns, which are an outline of what God will praise us for when we stand before Him in judgment.

The crown of righteousness (2 Tim. 4:7–8) is given to people who have demonstrated faithfulness, who have stood on the promises and joyously and constantly awaited the Lord's return. A reward for righteousness will be given to those who have maintained their perspective amidst all the faith-shattering circumstances of life. No matter what transpired, their final thought was always, "Jesus is coming again."

The crown of rejoicing (Phil. 4:1; 1 Thess. 2:19–20) is given to those who faithfully witness and share the gospel. This isn't just verbal witnessing but the witness of ongoing life service in the name of the Lord.

The crown of glory (1 Peter 5:4) is given to those who are faithful in the ministries in which God has placed them. It is given to those who use their gifts properly and fully and do not depart from the truth. This is a reward for actual performance, for doing works of faith.

The crown of life (Rev. 2:10; James 1:12) is given in praise for sacrificial obedience to those who have consistently endured temptation, persecution, suffering, and loss for Christ's sake.

The crown of incorruptibility (1 Cor. 9:25–27) is conferred for practicing purity in daily life. God bestows it on those who exercise self-control, rebuke the flesh, and live temperate lives.

Practicing the Principle of Servanthood

Although those rewards await us in the future, they can serve a practical purpose in the present. They are a composite of attributes the Lord Jesus Christ wants His servants to possess—keeping the faith, joyously anticipating His return, witnessing with our words and lives, doing works of faith in His name, obeying in the midst of even the most trying circumstances, and being holy.

We have "heard" that a Christian's entire life is a ministry and that the essence of ministry is sacrificial service. Now, we must "do." But where do we start?

Let's look to the perfect biblical example of a godly woman to get some pointers.

THREE

The Priscilla Principle

*"Charm is deceitful and beauty is vain,
but a woman who fears the Lord, she
shall be praised. Give her the product
of her hands, and let her works praise
her in the gates"*
PROV. 31:30–31.

Priscilla was exhausted. She and her husband, Aquila, and
their beloved friend Paul had been cutting and stitching the
heavy cilice since dawn. But she was too stimulated to sleep;
her mind was reeling from the words Paul had shared about
the Messiah. Tired as she was, she wished they could have
talked all night. Paul knew so many new and exciting things
about the Lord. She was hungry to hear them all. How she
wished she could have had the same kind of personal encounter with Him as had Paul on the road to Damascus. Hearing
him tell the story of the crystal, pure light from heaven flash-
ing around him and the Lord speaking his name aloud was
almost as good as having it happen to her.

She'd had numerous regrets when she and Aquila had first
come to Corinth. They hadn't left Rome by choice but had
been forced out of their native land by the mentally deranged
emperor, Claudius. No one was quite sure why he had exiled

the Jews. Some said it was on a whim—because his wife had asked him to prove his love for her by sending them out of the country. Others claimed it had been a show of power, to gain the respect of his subjects since he was such an inconsequential, weak ruler. It hadn't been easy for her to leave behind many of her dear friends and her possessions. After praying and weighing the alternatives, she and Aquila had chosen Corinth because it was a major seaport and trade center and was alive with activity and business opportunities. They agreed it was a city in which they could make a living, tentmaking.

But Corinth was a hotbed of immorality. Many citizens worshiped Aphrodite, the goddess of love and beauty. Prostitution, venereal disease, drunkenness, and gluttony were rampant. Even many of the Christians in Corinth were caught up in some type of heathen behavior. Living in Corinth was not easy for Priscilla. She worked long hours and struggled to make new friends and set up a home with what little she and Aquila had salvaged from Rome. Then, something miraculous happened. The apostle Paul came to Corinth. He stayed with them in their home and worked with them as a fellow tentmaker. When he arrived, Priscilla felt he was a gift sent to her by God. At times she felt like Christ Himself was with them, as she and Paul talked, prayed, studied, broke bread, and labored together.

As she, Aquila, and Paul labored side by side, both as tentmakers and in the Lord's work, the three of them became intimate friends. Paul became Priscilla's intellectual mentor and teacher, as well as beloved companion. He fondly referred to her as "Prisca," the nickname he had given her. Priscilla learned a new dimension of Christ's teaching from Paul and the more she learned, the more she longed to pass on to others what she had heard. So, she and Aquila became fellow-workers with the apostle Paul. They started holding services in their home, and Priscilla had opportunity, on many occasions, to develop her outstanding teaching ability.

After about a year and a half the Holy Spirit directed Paul to move on to Syria, then Ephesus. Priscilla and Aquila decided to accompany him. Unlike the move from Rome, the decision to follow Paul wasn't a difficult one. They wanted to go wherever they could be used by the Lord, and upon their arrival at Ephesus they immediately started a church in their new home. Priscilla was excited that she was again able to teach God's Word. In Ephesus, she devoted more and more of her time and energy to the cause of Christ.

When Paul left Ephesus to go to Palestine, she and her husband stayed behind. They loved Paul as much as they loved their own lives and were grieved at having to bid him good-by, yet they knew the Lord wanted them to remain in Ephesus. Their work with the church there was more important than their personal wishes. Still, it was a sad day when their friend departed.

In A.D. 54 they received the news that the emperor, Claudius, had died. They hastened back to their beloved Rome, where they once again established a church in their home. When Paul wrote to the brothers and sisters in that city, he included a special greeting for them. "Greet Prisca and Aquila, my fellow workers in Christ Jesus, who for my life risked their own necks, to whom not only do I give thanks, but also all the churches of the Gentiles. Also greet the church that is in their house" (Rom. 16:3–5). Priscilla's eyes filled with tears when she read his tender, warm words. She shuddered, recalling the time the angry mob, which had been worshiping Aphrodite, had chased him for denouncing her as a false god. They had been crazed with rage and drunkenness and, when Paul rushed to their home for shelter, she and Aquila had hidden him under a pile of tent cloth. The crowd had been so furious when they had not found Paul that they had dragged her and Aquila into the street, hitting and spitting on them. But Paul's safety was all that had mattered to them.

Her zeal did not diminish when, once again, she and her husband were forced to leave Rome, this time fleeing from the tyrannical emperor Nero, who was gleefully persecuting Christians—having them tortured and executed for refusing to denounce their faith. She knew in her heart that God was sending them back to Ephesus to minister.

Priscilla not only *lived* for the furtherance of the gospel; tradition says she and Aquila also died for their faith, that they were beheaded in Rome. Their beloved Paul, too, died under Nero's rule, but Priscilla's legacy of ministry has endured through the ages. Secular history and Scripture attest to her faith and performance. She was loved, accepted, and respected by both men and women. She worked alongside men, even one as forceful as Paul, as an equal in ministry. We cannot skim over her contribution to Christianity nor dismiss her as an exception in God's scheme for women. Instead, she should serve as a prototype, the first of a kind, but certainly not the last or only. She is an example and affirmation of our calling as sacrificial servants. Her life is a positive pattern after which we should model ourselves. We can develop many concepts about ministry from studying her life.

Sacrificial Servant

Priscilla was an exciting, talented woman—feminine yet dynamic and competent, in many ways the New Testament equivalent of the Proverbs 31 woman who epitomizes us all. She possessed many admirable qualities, most notably she was a *sacrificial servant*. She gave up many things that were and are important to any woman and was willing to make multiple concessions for the cause of Christ. She relinquished her home and the security of a permanent residence to travel with her husband and Paul and to spread the gospel. Today, when we move from one city to another or one house to another we can rent a U-drive truck or call a moving company and have the work done for us. Any losses we incur are covered by insurance. Priscilla traveled on dusty, dangerous roads, using beasts of burden to carry the few belongings she was able to take with her. When she and Aquila went with Paul to Syria they made the trip by sea. In those days ships were not luxury liners. There were no modern toilet facilities, and surely the boat carried a variety of bugs and rodents. Meals consisted of fish and tiny portions of dried fruit. Pirates roamed the waters, killing men for plunder and kidnaping women to sell into slavery. Yet Priscilla went, not to make a name for herself or to attain a position of leadership, but to serve Jesus Christ to the limits of her ability and endurance.

She also must have sacrificed her privacy. She had a church in her home in Corinth, Ephesus, and Rome. The early church didn't meet just for an hour or two on Sunday, as we do. The meeting of believers in those foundational days was truly a time of ongoing fellowship. Acts 2:42–46 shows that hosting a church in those days was much like holding a continual open house. Imagine the time and effort she must have expended in preparation of food alone. I'm sure she had help, but, nevertheless, it was her home and she was primarily responsible for her guests.

At one point in time, she and Aquila were ready to lay down their lives, if necessary, to assure Paul's safety. He, and all the churches of the Gentiles, thanked them publicly for risking their lives for his sake. Obviously, she wasn't afraid of the persecution the early Christians faced or of loss of status, because she was very open about her relationship with the church, her beloved friend Paul, and the Lord.

Yet, as I read about Priscilla, I get the distinct impression that she never thought of anything she did in terms of sacrifice or what she was giving up. I think she looked at the dangers and challenges she faced, at the hardships she endured, as an adventure with a predetermined happy ending—eternal life in Christ.

Devoted Wife

Like her unnamed sister in Proverbs 31, Priscilla was a devoted wife. "The heart of her husband trusts in her and he will have no lack of gain. She does him good and not evil all the days of her life" (Prov. 31:11–12). We can assume that Priscilla was such a wife. She co-labored with her husband both in tentmaking and the church. That she was so mightily and consistently used is a testimony to both her and Aquila and the quality of their relationship.

We can infer from Scripture that Priscilla and Aquila were extremely close, not only in activity, but emotionally. They understood and appreciated each other. They had an intriguing marriage. History and the words of Scripture indicate that Aquila was known as Priscilla's husband. The Holy Spirit set aside all cultural writing conventions, for, in Scripture, her name is listed before his, three times out of five. Paul referred to Aquila and Priscilla as "fellow workers," which means he looked upon them as equals. They must have viewed each other that way, too. Some theologians believe that Priscilla ministered under the auspices and direction of Aquila. In his book *The Apostle Paul and Women in the Church*, Don Williams affirms, "Nowhere is it suggested Prisca is inferior to or under the authority of Aquila in ministry. To the contrary, she shares a title and task of equality as a 'fellow-worker.' She is a fellow-worker in suffering and in church building and is universally recognized as such" (p. 43).

Priscilla's and Aquila's marriage shows how marriage can enhance Christian ministry for both spouses. They accepted and appreciated each other as individuals, then labored together as joint heirs of the grace of God. It illustrates that ministering *with* your husband doesn't mean ministering *under* him. Certainly, they were supportive of each other's ministries, but nothing in Scripture infers that Priscilla sought or needed Aquila's permission to do what God had called her to do. He didn't "let" her minister. He was a godly man who obviously wanted his wife to be obedient to the task God had set before her.

This particular facet of Priscilla's life has had special meaning to me. For whatever sovereign reason, God chose to give me a ministry in the foreground and my husband a ministry behind the scenes. We both serve and use our gifts, but in very different ways. We have been invited to "come as a couple" and teach a class or conduct a seminar. We tried that several times, but it didn't take us long to realize it doesn't work. God did not deem that we work in unison, but that we be supportive teammates. We readily seek one another's counsel but neither of us tries to tell the other what to do. We've learned to leave that up to the Lord. I am supportive of George's ministry and he is supportive of mine, but I don't serve under him, any more than he works under me. He doesn't ask my permission before he accepts a position on a board or committee and I don't ask his before I accept a speaking engagement, take a teaching assignment, or write a book. He doesn't "let" me teach or travel but encourages me to follow the Lord's leading and the dictates of my own conscience. He trusts me, just as Aquila must have trusted Priscilla, to do what is best for him and our marriage.

Risk-Taker

Being a Christian in the early church was dangerous. The governing authorities, the Gentiles, and the religious Jews all hated the Christians. In many ways, to declare oneself a follower of Christ was to accumulate a wide circle of enemies. The purity of the disciples' lives was a silent indictment of the heathens who engaged in all sorts of sexual immorality and illegal business practices. The Christians' total allegiance and obedience to their resurrected Lord was an affront to the ruling authorities, and their faith in Christ as the promised Messiah was an offensive stumbling block to the unsaved Hebrews. Believers were bombarded by opposition and persecution from all sides. Some were actually killed. The more vocal and visible a Christian was, the greater his or her chance of being harmed.

Priscilla was willing to risk her safety and security to put her faith into action. She was courageous. She wasn't merely involved with the church; her home *was* a well-known church. She had very little material security, but was blessed with a man who deeply loved her. Apparently, she was never comfortable with the status-quo, but thrived on living her life on the growing edge of her faith. She wasn't reckless, merely unconcerned, and she was willing to step out, undaunted, into the unknown for the sake of her Lord.

Organizer

When I think of how I get bogged down in what I consider a busy schedule (when I have all sorts of conveniences), I wonder how Priscilla accomplished what she did. She was a busy woman by any standard, yet she operated and managed her household well. Like the Proverbs 31 woman, she did not eat the bread of idleness (v. 27). Skilled in her profession, she worked as a tentmaker. She traveled. She helped form new churches, which is much more involved than playing hostess. She was also a teacher, which means she had to spend time studying. She was an outstanding example of what a dedicated, organized person can accomplish. Within a year after Paul committed his work in Ephesus to her and Aquila, they had set up a well-organized, highly-respected congregation. There is no doubt in my mind that she was gifted in the area of administration, but I believe another secret to her success was that she diligently pursued whatever needed to be done. She wasn't worried about who did what but simply noted needs and found a way to meet them. She must have been able to recognize giftedness in others, too, and assign tasks and delegate authority.

Hospitable

Another of Priscilla's gifts was hospitality. Hospitality is listed and exemplified throughout Scripture as an admirable trait and means *to entertain strangers with love.* Priscilla certainly did that. When Paul, a stranger to her, came to Corinth, he sought out Priscilla and Aquila because they were all tentmakers (Acts 18:3). She and Aquila warmly welcomed him into their midst as a brother. It seems that Priscilla was very people-oriented and had a talent for making them feel at ease and comfortable in her home.

When you study Priscilla's ministry, it is easy to understand why the Spirit gifted her in this area. God structured her life so others could come to her, so she could reach out through her home. She could not have been used as effectively by the Lord if she had not been hospitable—willing to give room and board to strangers and to welcome them into her home without reservation.

We must not forget that Priscilla's house was also a church. If we are to follow Priscilla's example, we need to entertain strangers with love in our churches as well as in our homes. Recently I saw a perfect example of godly hospitality. We visited a church where first-time, Sunday-morning visitors were invited into the homes of various members for lunch. I was so impressed by the warmth expressed in these on-the-spot invitations that I asked a deacon after the service how most visitors react to such hospitality. He told me over half of them accept and that others take a raincheck. "But," he added, "we don't care how many people accept. We just want them to know we love them and are glad they came to worship with us. We want them to feel welcome in our fellowship."

Many churches ask visitors to fill out cards or stand and be introduced or shake hands with people around them, but how many go beyond that? Sometimes guests are never noticed or spoken to by any of the regular attenders. I wonder how successful the church in Priscilla's and Aquila's home would have been if its members had been as reclusive as we tend to be. Hospitality within the body is as necessary today as it was in the early church.

Strong

Priscilla possessed both physical vitality and strength of character. "She [girded] herself with strength and [made] her arms strong" (Prov. 31:17). We have already discussed that she was an ardent worker who labored diligently both at her trade and in ministry. Her abilities and circumstances required a great deal of physical stamina and emotional equilibrium. She was, as Scripture says, clothed in both strength and dignity. She was fiercely loyal. She stood by Paul in the face of great danger and pursued her calling with an unwavering faith and zeal. She had to have been enthusiastic because she motivated people with her words and her sacrificial life. She gave up material possessions, social standing, and the security of a permanent residence to serve Christ. That kind of dedication takes strength of character and deep conviction.

Today, we hear a lot about burnout, a psychological term that means a person has overdone to the point of mental and physical exhaustion. Many experts contend that burnout is stress, rather than activity, related.

When I study about people like Paul and Priscilla I wonder why they didn't suffer from burnout. Couldn't we assume that after Priscilla and Aquila had to leave Rome for a second time and move back to Ephesus that they had had all they could stand and should have dropped out for a while? Couldn't we say that, after Paul had been thrown in prison and survived numerous threats on his life, he needed some time off? Priscilla, Aquila, and Paul suffered tribulation, distress, persecution, famine, nakedness, bodily harm and death threats (see Rom. 8:35), but they never suffered from burnout. They lived by the truth, "I can do all things through [Christ] who strengthens me " (Phil. 4:13).

Why, when we don't labor as hard or under nearly as severe circumstances as they, do we collapse under the strain?

From my own experience (I burned out in 1979), I conclude it is because we are not living our lives as ministries. We get sidetracked into working for causes or organizing projects or serving the church or holding positions on committees and end up serving institutions or people rather than the Lord. We get so busy doing things for Him that we lose sight of Him. We start ministering out of duty or because it's expected of us or because our role requires it. I know firsthand that living like that is spiritually, emotionally, and physically debilitating. When that happens, we are operating out of God's will. On a daily or moment-by-moment basis, we may be doing His bidding, but in the general manner in which we're living, we are not. We become misplaced persons and eventually joy decreases, zeal diminishes, satisfaction stops, and motivation fades. We burn out and blame our "overserving," when in reality we were doing the wrong things for the wrong reasons. The only way to avoid spiritual burnout is to live as Priscilla did: She made her whole life a ministry so wherever she was, she was serving the Lord according to His will.

Devoted Disciple

Priscilla, a devoted disciple, was famous and respected by early Christian writers. One of the oldest catacombs of Rome, the Coemeterium Priscilla, is named after her, as is the church "Titulus Saint Prisca" on the Aventine in her native city of Rome. The preservation of her name and ministry both by secular historians and by the Holy Spirit in Scripture is proof of her stature. Gien Karssen, in her book *Her Name Is Woman*, notes that Priscilla's prominence is evidenced by her having taught the learned and eloquent Apollos, by the church assembling in her home, and her being known throughout the first-century Christian community. But Priscilla wasn't loved and respected because she was pretty or charming or a good hostess. Like the godly woman in Proverbs 31, she was revered and honored because of her works (vv. 30–31). Priscilla received praise and recognition because she feared the Lord.

The way Priscilla lived reflected that she truly adored and worshiped the Lord. She didn't have to prove her Christianity to anyone; the product of her hands, the fruits of her labor, validated her faith. Although she was a gifted teacher, her godly example, rather than fancy words, was the foundation for the praise that was lavished on her. She understood that being a Christian means going and showing, not sitting and telling. She was an authentic disciple who tried in every way to imitate Christ. He was so real to her that His presence permeated every word she said, every act she performed.

A few weeks ago I was watching a television interview with

a well-known impersonator. The host of the show asked him how he manages to look and sound so much like other people, how he transforms himself into someone else. He explained that he first spends hours studying film of the person he is going to mimic. He memorizes physical gestures and personal characteristics. Next, he listens to voice tapes so he can isolate speech inflections and imitate the way his subject phrases words. "I literally become that person. I totally submerge myself in him. I try to think like he thinks, mirror his attitudes, say what he would say, and move as he would move."

In the same way, we must totally submerge ourselves in Christ. We must try to think as He thinks, mirror His attitudes, say what He would say, and act as He would act. We must study Him in detail, constantly perusing the Gospels to keep His example fresh in our minds. We must ingrain His ideas, His responses, His attitudes into our hearts, Then we will become dedicated disciples like Priscilla.

Student-Teacher of the Word

Priscilla was also a gifted teacher. Evidence indicates that she may well have been a preacher in the early church. The historian Tertullian wrote, "By the holy Prisca, the Gospel is preached." Coupled with statements such as the one by Tertullian is the fact that a church was named after her and that the Roman Catholic church has set aside a day to honor her ministry. In her book, *Wisdom from Women in the Bible,* Edith Deen notes that "Although Priscilla and Aquila walked side by side in all they did, Priscilla was probably the more profound teacher of the two" (p. 146).

Whether teacher or preacher, she lived a life of purity that was becoming to the Lord and was competent and efficient in the execution of her ministry. But, she would not have been proficient if she had not been a learned student of the Word. Every teacher knows you simply cannot pass on to others what you don't know. Priscilla's first intimate insights about Christ probably came from the apostle Paul, passed on to her as they talked and labored side by side when he lived with her and Aquila in Corinth. I imagine she pumped him for detailed information, hoping to satisfy her insatiable appetite for God's truth. She hungered and thirsted after righteousness—questioning, reading, listening, ever eager to gain better understanding and gather more information about her Savior. That knowledge was reflected in the bold, effective way she ministered.

Priscilla learned in an era when women were considered intellectual inferiors and were denied education. In religious matters, most wives were addenda to their husband's faith. That was not so with Priscilla. She must have studied arduously, laboring over the Scriptures, searching and probing, devouring truth, struggling to rightly divide the Word. She didn't have the total text of Scripture or research books and Bible dictionaries and atlases and concordances; she relied on her memory and intelligence and her innate ability to discern the Old Testament writings and Paul's teaching. Yet, her learning was thorough and correct.

Although Scripture doesn't spell out in exact detail how Priscilla and Aquila handled the day-to-day details of their setting up and running the churches they established, it does give us a specific example of how they taught. Acts 18:24–26 records the story of an encounter they had with an Egyptian Jew, Apollos. He was an Old Testament scholar, a sort of traveling preacher, and probably had come to Ephesus for the explicit purpose of teaching there. He was an eloquent man who knew how to use language correctly and to convince others with his words. He also was "mighty in the Scriptures" (Acts 18:24). He had a full command of the Old Testament and knew how to use and apply it, as well as teach it to others, which he did with great zeal and fervor. "This man had been instructed in the way of the Lord, and being fervent in spirit, he was speaking and teaching accurately the things concerning Jesus (v. 25).

Priscilla and Aquila heard Apollos teaching in the synagogue. Possibly, they had gone just to hear him, but they were bothered by the content of his teaching. What he taught, he taught accurately, but, as brilliant and learned as Apollos was, his teaching was incomplete. He obviously had not heard the full gospel story. He was still teaching about John the Baptist preparing the way of the Lord. It appears that he believed that Jesus was the Messiah but he didn't know about Christ's death and resurrection, and certainly not about the coming of the Spirit at Pentecost. Considering he was from Egypt, such a lack of information was possible. While his ignorance in no way reflected on his ability, his teaching was incomplete and therefore erroneous. So, "When Priscilla and Aquila heard him, they took him aside and explained to him the way of God more accurately" (v. 26).

Several things about Priscilla's teaching stand out in this story. First, we see her authority and her knowledge. She didn't urge Aquila to talk to Apollos; since her name is mentioned first we might assume she initiated the endeavor. She approached him as an equal with her husband and had no qualms about correcting a man who was both an Old Testament scholar and noted teacher. She, with her husband, divided the word "more accurately" to him. They taught Apollos things he didn't know and added to his comprehension with a detailed, careful, complete, precise, accurate account of the gospel.

Another thing we see about Priscilla's teaching is that she was tactful. She and Aquila took Apollos aside. They could have interrupted him when he was teaching and questioned him publicly, detracting from his dignity and respect and downgrading his authority. Instead, they talked with him privately. That gesture says more about their character than anything I could elaborate. It shows that, as a godly teacher, Priscilla was more interested in seeing that the Word of God was taught correctly than in elevating her status by putting down a man like Apollos. Like her sister in Proverbs 31, "she [opened] her mouth in wisdom, and the teaching of kindness [was] on her tongue" (v. 26).

This passage also reveals that Priscilla was an encourager. She and Aquila did not demean or judge Apollos because he had not yet heard the entire gospel. Instead, they kindly and successfully corrected error. What could have been a humiliating experience was turned into a positive one, for Apollos went on to become a preacher in the early church. In no small way, he was "fruit" from Priscilla's ministry.

The Priscilla Principle

No woman in the New Testament ministered more zealously or effectively than Priscilla. We can draw several conclusions from her life. The first is that she viewed her entire life as a ministry dedicated to her Lord Jesus Christ. Everything she did, whether as homemaker, wife, teacher, or friend, was an outcropping of her Christianity. Christ was her primary focus, her first love, the prominent, abiding center of her existence. She was, in the fullest sense, a sacrificial servant.

Second, she understood that the call to ministry is to all believers and is not determined by a person's sex or marital status. Abraham Kuyper observes that "From her position in the Word of God she affirms that a woman, also a married woman, has another calling besides those of dispatching daily duties and engaging in activities of mercy" (*Women of the*

New Testament, p. 103). Her sex and marital status seem to be irrelevant, unrelated to her performance and its effectiveness. Interestingly, Scripture never recounts encounters she had with other women, only the way she co-labored with her husband and men such as Paul and Apollos.

Third, Priscilla looked to the Lord for direction in ministry. She interpreted Scripture in the light of the leading of the Spirit and served in areas in which He gifted her. She responded to the opportunities He presented her and didn't get all hung up about what would please other church leaders or what was proper or expected of her or acceptable for a woman to do. She took personal responsibility for defining and completing her life's ministry.

With her as our model, we can develop a principle for ministry, which I call *The Priscilla Principle*. Simply stated, I believe: *Every facet of each Christian woman's life must be looked upon as an ongoing ministry, dedicated to the Lord Jesus Christ. What she does should be determined by the leading of the Holy Spirit, her giftedness, and the opportunities for service that God sets in her paths. She must take personal responsibility for defining God's will and developing a theology of ministry based on a thorough knowledge of the Scriptures.*

Priscilla knew, understood, and lived by that principle, and as a result lived a dynamic, fulfilling life which brought honor and glory to God. The same thing is possible for Christian women today. But before we can practice the principle, we need to plug into the right power source.

FOUR

God's Provision: Serving With Power

*"You shall receive power when the
Holy Spirit has come upon you"*
ACTS 1:8.

Several years ago, when George, the children, and I were visiting in the Midwest, we went to church with my cousin and her family. The church to which they then belonged was quite liberal so I was intrigued by the sermon title: Who Is the Holy Spirit? The regular pastor was away that Sunday and his new, young associate, who was filling the pulpit, preached for thirty minutes. I listened carefully. He definitely stuck to his theme; he would make some observation about the Holy Spirit (none based on Scripture so I assume the ideas were his own), then ask, "Who is the Holy Spirit?" The problem was, he never answered the question.

Many Christians are like that young pastor; they are dangerously ignorant about the role and purpose of the Spirit in their lives, yet He is God's power-provision to us, the One who enables us to minister effectively and live purely. Being

58

the third person of the Holy Trinity, He is God—equal with the Father and Son—and works in perfect unity with Them. He possesses the same attributes as they. He is Love and Truth. He is just, holy, righteous, omniscient, omnipresent, omnipotent, sovereign, faithful, and gracious. He is the unique inner working of God's person, personality, and power in every believer. He is God's promise of His presence in our lives.

The promise of the Spirit was made both at the commencement and conclusion of Christ's earthly ministry. When Jesus was baptized by John (Mark 1:10–11), The Holy Spirit, in the form of a dove, came upon Jesus as an indication that He was supernaturally equipped with all of the gifts and the power to accomplish His task as Redeemer of sinful humanity. The Holy Spirit's descent was an example to us: if Jesus, as a man, was dependent on the Holy Spirit in His ministry, so must we be. We cannot live like Jesus—or like Priscilla—without the help of the Holy Spirit.

At the conclusion of Christ's ministry Christ's followers were promised the power and presence of the Holy Spirit. Jesus' final vow to His disciples before He ascended to the Father was "You shall receive power when the Holy Spirit has come upon you" (Acts 1:8). There is no doubt that the Holy Spirit is intrinsic to a successful, fruitful Christian life.

The Coming of the Spirit

The clearest, best doctrinal teaching about the Holy Spirit was done by Jesus Christ, when He was instructing and praying for His disciples immediately before His crucifixion. At that time He shared with them some of the most dramatically different, life-altering concepts found in the Bible. Hoping to prepare them to carry on His work when He was gone, Jesus taught them about the Holy Spirit. If we are going to serve with power, we also need to understand better these foundational truths about the third He, who makes His home in the temple of our earthly bodies.

Jesus understood that His disciples, His inseparable, close friends of almost three years, were confused by what was happening. They didn't want Him to die. They were afraid of being without Him. He was their Leader, their Strength, the One who gave purpose, direction, and meaning to their lives. To allay their fears, Jesus promised, "I will ask the Father, and He will give you another helper, that He may be with you forever" (John 14:16). Surely, those words must have consoled them. Jesus wasn't deserting them, but sending Someone in His place, Someone who would *never* leave them. A Christian's relationship with the Spirit is irrevocable. We are eternally secure, "sealed in [Christ] with the Holy Spirit of promise, who is given as a pledge of our inheritance" (Eph. 1:13–14). The Holy Spirit seals our salvation. He is God's pledge to us that we will inherit a place in the kingdom of God. Knowing that God will never withdraw from our lives frees us to serve with power.

Jesus also taught that the Holy Spirit comes to us as a result of His requesting it of the Father, not because of anything we say or do. Each of us who belongs to Him through faith receives the Spirit (Rom. 8:9). All Christians are indwelt by the Spirit, endowed with God's power source. There is no salvation apart from the presence of the Spirit. The baptism of the Spirit isn't about signs, gifts, and wonders but about power and our immersion into oneness with our Lord.

God the Father is the source of the Holy Spirit. Christ asks and the Father sends. The Holy Spirit obviously chooses to act in submission and accordance with the Father's will, just as Christ did. Therefore, when we follow the leading of the Spirit, we are also in the center of God's will.

Knowing that His disciples felt frightened and impotent

without Him, Jesus referred to the Spirit as a Helper. In the Greek, that word means *an aide; someone who comes along side and upholds, who offers consolation and comfort, who encourages and erases grief, who intervenes on our behalf, protecting our welfare.* Christ had been that kind of Helper to His disciples, and in a very real sense the Holy Spirit was and is a replacement for Christ. The Holy Spirit upholds us when we start to fall, consoles and comforts us when we are hurting, and encourages us when we are downhearted.

The Indwelling of the Spirit

Next, the Lord explained a change that was going to occur when the Helper arrived. He said the world (unregenerate sinners, unbelievers) couldn't receive the Spirit of Truth "because it does not behold Him or know Him but you know Him because He abides *with* you and will be *in* you" (John 14:17). The Holy Spirit didn't permanently indwell believers until Pentecost. In the Old Testament, the Spirit was given when God counted someone righteous through faith and empowered him or her to do God's bidding. This "coming upon" was temporary and was given to equip the person for service, not to assure a right relationship with God.

If you recall, when King David fell in contrite confession before God, after he had committed adultery with Bathsheba and used his position as commander of the Israelite army to murder her husband, he prayed, "Do not cast me away from Thy presence and do not take Thy Holy Spirit from me" (Ps. 51:11). He knew his sin could cause him to lose the Spirit.

But Christ told His disciples that the Holy Spirit was *with* them and eventually would be *in* them. This was a revolutionary idea, which we take for granted. The thought of being indwelt permanently by the presence and power of God through His Spirit must have boggled the minds of those twelve men. It should boggle ours. Think about what having God within us means. The same God who shut the mouths of the lions to protect Daniel, who healed the sick with but a word or a touch, who resurrected the dead, who revolutionized the lives of hopeless adulterers such as the woman at the well, thieves such as Zaccheus, and murderers such as Paul lives in us. Imagine what we could do if we consistently lived that reality.

Receiving the Spirit

After promising the indwelling of the Spirit, Jesus explained the conditions for receiving His permanent placement in our souls. "If anyone loves Me, He will keep My word and My Father will love Him and We will come to him and make Our abode with Him" (John 14:23). Christ set forth two conditions for receiving the Spirit: loving Him and keeping His word. The love He asks from us is not some superficial, emotional reaction but the unconditional, irreversible, committed *agape* love. Obeying His teaching is more than simple obedience to the law. It is complete, unconditional surrender to all He asks and personal acceptance and confession of every truth about Him, as is historically identified in the Apostles' Creed.

Jesus' instruction to His disciples made it abundantly clear that the only conditions for receiving the Holy Spirit are love and obedience. Nowhere in the Bible are we told to ask for the Spirit. Jesus said the Spirit is sent by the Father when a person commits to the lordship of Christ through a faith-love relationship. His coming is an automatic love response to our surrender, and once He arrives He makes His home or abode with us. In the Greek, *abode* means *a permanent dwelling place*, once again implying an unending liaison. It is then up to us to make a comfortable home for the Holy Spirit by living holy lives.

Our Spiritual Teacher

After the Lord outlined the conditions for receiving the Spirit, He explained the Spirit's role. "The Helper, the Holy Spirit, whom the Father will send in my name, He will teach you all things and bring to your remembrance all that I said to you" (John 14:26). Christ mentioned two specific functions the Spirit performs in the life of a believer. He teaches us spiritual truth. We cannot comprehend it without Him because "a natural man does not accept the things of the Spirit of God, for they are foolishness to him, and he cannot understand them, because they are spiritually appraised" (1 Cor. 2:14). The Spirit awakens our spiritual understanding and illuminates the Word of God. He is our initial and primary teacher, who interprets Scripture to us and shows us how to apply it. He is also our spiritual memory bank. He stores Jesus' words in that miraculous computer, the human brain, then recalls them as needed. We have seen how He did this in Priscilla's life; He can also do it in ours.

I once witnessed an amazing example of this inner-working of the Spirit. When I was still teaching school, I took various classes to upgrade my skills. In one of them, "Educating the Exceptional Child," we visited an institution for retarded adults. Each student was assigned a person with whom to spend time. We were to interview this person and note skills he or she had learned. The twenty-three-year-old man with whom I met was able to write his name and address, recite his telephone number, and walk three blocks to the grocery store and back. He read at a first-grade level, but with very little comprehension. Talking with him was like talking with a four-year-old.

When the supervisor came up to us, she said, "Gary, why don't you say some of your Bible verses for Mrs. Berry."

Immediately, his face brightened and he asked, "Do you love Jesus?" Before I could answer, he explained the entire salvation message to me. He quoted the King James John 3:16, John 1:12, and Revelation 3:20. He recited the entire Twenty-third Psalm. This, from a man who could barely remember his phone number and couldn't recite the alphabet or memorize addition facts! He had a spiritual understanding far beyond his natural mental capabilities. There is not a doubt in my mind that he was illuminated by the indwelling presence of the Holy Spirit.

A Truthful Aide

Later, Christ stated a second function the Spirit performs in our lives. "When the Helper comes, whom I will send to you from the Father, that is the Spirit of Truth, who proceeds from the Father, He will bear witness of Me; and you will bear witness also, because you have been with Me from the beginning" (John 15:26–27). Isn't it interesting that Jesus repeated so much of what He had said before: that the Spirit is a Helper, that He is sent by the Father at Christ's request, and, for the third time, He referred to the Spirit as the Spirit of Truth.

The Holy Spirit has many scriptural titles. He is called the Spirit of Christ, the Spirit of Jesus Christ, the Spirit of Jesus, the Spirit of God, the Spirit of His Son, the Spirit of the Lord, the Spirit of Jehovah, the Spirit of the Lord God, the Spirit of the Father, and the Spirit of the living God. These titles reveal the beautiful, inseparability of the triune God, how the Father, Son, and Holy Spirit are inextricably melded in one Being—Elohim.

When Christ taught about the Spirit, He called Him the

Spirit of Truth. Truth is His essence and He is the source of perfect truth in our lives. He will never lie and never say or do anything that contradicts Scripture. The leading of the Spirit will always match the written Word of God. I remember a time when one of the women in a Bible study I was teaching announced that she was leaving her husband, who was an unbeliever, because God was leading her to marry a Christian. She had deluded herself into thinking that God wanted her to divorce her husband, who was a loving, moral man and good father, so she could marry a child of God. We spent hours going through Scripture, tracing how her actions were contradictory to some very specific commandments. She couldn't explain why the Spirit would lead her to commit adultery when Exodus 20:14 said, "Thou shalt not," yet she knew He was. It took months to convince her that she was rationalizing her sin. We must always be mindful that the Holy Spirit never leads us into temptation or to do anything that is out of accord with God's Word.

A Witness

Witnessing is another function of the Spirit. The Holy Spirit bears witness *in* us about Christ. He reveals Jesus to us— makes Him real, activates His presence, reminds us that we are His. The Spirit also bears witness about Christ *through* us, to others. He capacitates us to witness, as disciples of Christ, with our words and lives. The Holy Spirit testifies to us what He has seen, heard, and knows is true about Jesus. Then we minister to others by passing on that truth. We tell them what we have seen, heard and know is true about Jesus.

A Guide

The Spirit is also a personal guide. Jesus said, "When He, the Spirit of Truth, comes, He will guide you into all truth"

(John 16:13). Notice the word *all*, which includes more than just spiritual truth. Not all truth is contained in the Bible, but every word in the Bible is truth, and it is our measuring standard. As an additional help, the Holy Spirit directs us into other truth. He protects us from error.

When I was a child, my parents and I went on a tour of the Cave of the Winds, quite an ominous, awesome place. The guide warned us never to leave the path, to follow him at all times for our "pleasure and safety." He not only showed us where to go but told us where not to go. He knew the way, the dangers lurking in the nooks and crevices off the path. I was impressed enough to stay as close to him as I could because I didn't want to get hurt or lost. The Holy Spirit is our Guide, and we should follow Him—for our pleasure and safety.

Sometimes His guidance prevents us from doing something, from making mistakes or wrong decisions. When the apostle Paul was on one of his missionary journeys, the Spirit directed Paul's route by restraining his actions. He was "forbidden by the Holy Spirit to speak the word in Asia" and when he and Barnabas wanted to go to Bithynia, "the Spirit of Jesus did not permit them" (Acts 16:6–7). God's negative direction is actually positive, yet we usually carp and complain when plans get changed or things don't happen the way we want them to. The circumstances Priscilla faced illustrate the "negative" leading of the Spirit. His duty as our Guide is to restrain and direct. Ours is to respond and obey, just as Priscilla did, even in the face of adversity.

A Communicator

The Spirit also acts as the agent of communication between God and us. "He will not speak on His own initiative, but whatever He hears (John 16:13). The Holy Spirit is totally submissive to Christ. He communicates only what He hears from Him. He transmits Christ's thoughts, Christ's wishes, Christ's words, and Christ's presence to us.

When Jesus said the Holy Spirit would speak, He meant that in some way the Spirit would tell or show us God's truth and will for our lives. Jesus did not mean the Spirit would verbally converse with us. Actually, He speaks to us in several ways. He speaks through the pages of Scripture. Infrequently, He does speak in words to us, but He communicates to most people through thoughts—through the ideas and feelings He implants in minds. His leading is an intuitive confirmation or enlightenment, a flooding of peace coupled with a certainty of direction, and sometimes with specific knowledge. If you're a Christian, you've experienced it. We simply know when the Spirit "speaks," and when He does He is disclosing Christ to us.

Glorifying Christ

Jesus explained that the final purpose of the Holy Spirit is to glorify Christ. "He shall glorify Me, for He shall take of mine and disclose it to you" (John 16:14). This is why the Holy Spirit is not as predominant as the Father and the Son, why we don't hear or know as much about Him. God structured it that way. The Holy Spirit is the Person behind the scenes who orchestrates our lives from within. He purposely does not call attention to Himself but directs it toward Christ. He always defers to and points to Jesus.

The Filling of the Spirit

We have seen that all believers are indwelt by the Holy Spirit. He is the source of power for our ministries, but many times we short-circuit Him and render Him useless because of sin or indifference. I venture to say, none of us takes full advantage of the personal presence of the Holy Spirit. We're too busy doing our own thing to give Him full rein. We are all baptized (immersed in) and indwelt by the Spirit but we are not always controlled by or filled with Him. While His indwelling is an absolute (He is always with us), He does not always control us. We may or may not be filled with Him at any given moment.

Ephesians 5:18 commands us to be "filled with the Spirit." Here the word *filled* doesn't mean being filled up, like a glass with water or a tank with gas. The Holy Spirit isn't a liquid, He's a Person. Being filled with the Spirit means turning control of our lives over to Him, letting Him fill us like the wind fills the sails of a ship and propells it on its rightful course. The verb tense in this command tells us we are to keep on being filled continuously. Filling is not a once-and-for-all thing, like indwelling, but an ongoing, moment-by-moment process of surrender and submission of our will to the Spirit's desire. Dr. Alfred Martin of the Moody Bible Institute explains the filling of the Spirit this way: "A believer can never obtain more of the Holy Spirit, for He indwells the Christian's life in all His fullness. But the Holy Spirit can get more of the believer; that is, He can exercise complete control of the life that is yielded to Him."

There is no such thing as partial filling. Either we control our lives or the Spirit does. We can't be partially cleansed and partly sin-infested, a little bit righteous, or somewhat submissive to God's will. Either we are controlled by the Spirit or we are self-controlled.

What Is Filling?

Filling is, first and foremost, being "filled up to all the fullness of God" (Eph. 3:19). When we are full of the Spirit, we are controlled by God, and He manifests His attributes through us. Those rivers of living water of which Christ spoke flow from our innermost beings to quench the spiritual thirst of needy souls.

Finally, filling is acting out our positions in Christ. "The law of the Spirit of life in Christ Jesus has set you free from the law of sin and death" (Rom. 8:2). When we are Spirit-filled, we exercise our freedom not to sin. Before Christ, we were enslaved to sin. Every deed we performed, every thought we had, no matter how good or noble it seemed on the surface, was sin, because it was done apart from Christ. It was impossible for you not to sin. Christ freed us from that enslavement. Now, in Him, we have been granted the privilege of deciding whether or not to sin. We can choose. We can live as we did before or practice the holy, righteous position that is ours in Christ. When we let the Spirit control us, our earthly life-styles match our eternal positions.

How To Be Filled

We do not have to follow a set procedure to be Spirit-filled. It's not something for which we have to ask, but it comes when we release ourselves and our wills to God and give Him charge over our thoughts, actions, and words. When we usurp that control, we negate the filling.

Some people expect to get a special feeling when they are filled with the Spirit, and certainly there are times when His presence and leading are so dramatic and overwhelming that we are euphoric, but generally the only feeling generated by filling is a general sense of peace and well being. Being filled doesn't mean being on a continual spiritual "high." Filling is not a feeling but a fact. It was a fact with Priscilla. Her life attests that she was Spirit-filled. Unless a person is resting in the center of God's will by submitting to the control of His

Spirit, he or she cannot be used as mightily as Priscilla to reach others for Christ and effectively teach God's Word. Christ promised to send His Spirit, commanded us to be filled, and, when we do what He asks, He fills us.

Conditions for Filling

There are three biblical conditions for filling; two negatives, or "do nots," and one positive. The first is, "Do not grieve the Holy Spirit of God, by whom you were sealed for the day of redemption" (Eph. 4:30). When Christians sin, we grieve the person of the Holy Spirit. Because He is holy, the Spirit cannot participate in our sin, so when sin is present in the person He indwells, He must turn from His ministry *through* the believer and negotiate a pleading, convicting ministry *to* that person. Sin stops the God-flow. It eradicates power. The Holy Spirit remains when sin is present but He is repulsed and confined by it.

Grief—deep sorrow and distress of soul—is God's emotional response to our sin. The grief experienced by the Spirit is something like the despair and depression we experience when someone we love fails us or when impossible, irreconcilable differences drive us apart. It's like the pain a devoted wife endures when her husband tells her he doesn't love her any more and is leaving her for another woman. As the bride of Christ, when we sin, we leave our Lord to have an affair with evil. It's like the sorrow parents suffer when a beloved child goes against everything he or she has been taught and sets on a course of self-destruction. Sin is monumentally destructive in the life of God's children. The grief of the Spirit is similar to the despair people bear when a loved one dies; God hurts when someone who has been regenerated in Christ dies once again to sin.

But these earthly parallels cannot compare with the misery

the Holy Spirit bears as a result of our sin. In grace and love, He came to make His permanent home in our physical bodies, and, when we sin, He is trapped in the filth and garbage of evil. He must suffer immeasurably, much like Christ did on the cross when He took our sin upon Himself and cried out in agony, "My God, my God, why hast Thou forsaken Me?" (Matt. 27:46).

We should think long and often about how the presence of sin in our lives wounds the Holy Spirit. And we should realize what it does to us. Any sin that grieves and depresses the Holy Spirit also causes grief and depression in our human spirits. It weighs us down, saps our physical and spiritual strength, and causes guilt and frustration.

The command is "Do not grieve," but, if we do, we can relieve the oppression of sin by confession and repentance. "If we confess our sins, He is faithful and righteous to forgive us our sins and to cleanse us from all unrighteousness" (1 John 1:9). Confessing sin means more than admitting we've transgressed; it means agreeing with God that what we did was an affront to His holiness. Confession presupposes a sorrow for having sinned, a regret for having brought grief and heartache to the Spirit of God. Confession also implies a willingness to turn away from sin and not to repeat the infraction. When we approach God with that kind of broken heart and contrite spirit, fellowship is restored and filling occurs.

The second negative condition for the filling of the Spirit is, "Do not quench the Spirit" (1 Thess. 5:19). When we sin, we not only grieve the person of the Spirit but we quench His actions, or His movement in our lives. Quenching relates to the "fire" aspect of the Holy Spirit. In Scripture, the Spirit is, several times, likened to fire. At Pentecost, He was represented as tongues of fire to the disciples, then they were filled. John the Baptist said that Christ will "baptize you with the Holy Spirit and fire" (Matt. 3:11). The presence of the

Spirit creates a burning desire for God within believers and sets us on fire for the Lord.

Fire consumes. Anyone who has seen a brush or forest fire knows how rapidly it spreads and how completely it devours everything in its path. When we give the Spirit full rein, we are consumed by God and He uses our zeal and enthusiasm to draw others to Him. The Spirit keeps us "fired up"; He fuels our spirituality. Certainly Priscilla had that kind of consuming desire to serve the Lord. She was a pliable tool in His hands, eager to follow and obey.

Just as the flame on the burner of a stove goes out when the gas is turned off, and as a campfire stops burning when it is watered down or buried in dirt, so the fire of the Holy Spirit is quenched when we shut off our spiritual fuel supply by saying *no* to God. When we know the Lord is leading us to do something and we don't do it, we quench the Spirit. The fire of the Spirit is also quenched when we suffocate God's will by covering it with the dirt of sin or when we throw the cold water of disobedience on His holy desires for our lives.

Through obedience, we can reignite the fire of the Spirit. When we fuel God's moving with enthusiastic compliance to His nature, we live in harmony with Scripture, understand His will for us, and possess the supernatural power that is the fulfillment of the filling of the Spirit.

The third and positive condition for filling is "Walk by the Spirit, and you will not carry out the desires of the flesh" (Gal. 5:16). Remember, the Holy Spirit is our Guide, our Paraclete, who comes alongside to accompany and uphold us as we walk through life, and who, when we walk by Him, keeps us from sinning.

Walking by the Spirit means being propelled by Him, using Him as a spiritual vehicle to transport us along the road of life. When we visit our next-door neighbor, we go by foot. If we go to town, we go by car or bus. When we travel cross country, we go by plane and, if we walk the path of righteous-ness, we walk by the Spirit. Your walk is your lifestyle. The apostle John observed that "the one who says he abides in [Christ] ought himself to walk in the same manner as He walked" (1 John 2:6). Walking by the Spirit is living as Jesus lived, emulating His actions and attitudes. When we do, we are Spirit-filled.

When we freely and completely abandon ourselves to the Spirit, exciting things happen: We speak "to one another in psalms and hymns and spiritual songs, singing and making melody with [our] hearts to the Lord, always giving thanks to God, even the Father for all things in the name of our Lord Jesus Christ" (Eph. 5:19–20). And, when we walk by the Spirit, God produces fruit in our lives.

The Fruit of the Spirit

The fruit of the Spirit is a by-product of the filling of the Spirit. It is the crop of righteousness the Holy Spirit cultivates and grows in our lives when we belong to Christ. It is the manifestation of the filling and presence of the Holy Spirit. "The fruit of the Spirit is love, joy, peace, long-suffering, gentleness, goodness, faith, meekness, temperance: against such there is no law," (Gal. 5:22–23). These Christlike traits are both a personal blessing and a witness to others. The fruit the Spirit produces is evidence of the distinct contrast be-tween the world's way of reacting to and approaching life and God's way. When we are filled with the Spirit, the deeds of the Spirit are evident in our lives and entice others, providing opportunities to share the gospel with them. Christians are indwelt by the Spirit so He can empower us to live divinely different lives—lives in which God dominates our minds, emotions, wills and actions, and through which His love con-tinuously flows. But God doesn't merely want us to be different for our personal pleasure and satisfaction; He wants others to notice how different we are. The fruit of the Spirit is evidence of God's power, an external validation of His presence in the lives of His children, drawing others to us so we can minister to them. Fruit is proof to unbelievers that we are empowered by a supernatural God. But fruit isn't merely something we have or produce; it is something we experience emotionally. When we respond in *faith* to the *facts* in God's Word and claim the *filling* of the Spirit, He produces *fruit* in our lives; then we experience *feelings*. Each fruit is accompanied by a positive, edifying emotion.

Love

The foundational fruit of the Spirit is love. This is God's agape love, generated by the One who loves, and not dependent on anything the recipient says or does. God loved us before we were saved: "God demonstrates His own love toward us in that while we were yet sinners, Christ died for us" (Rom. 5:8), and He loves us now. "See how great a love the Father has bestowed upon us, that we should be called Children of God" (1 John 3:1). Love produced by the Spirit is unconditional love. It says, "I love you," not "I love you because . . . ," or I'll love you if. . . ." The realization that God accepts and values us, just as we are, and that we don't have to do anything to win or maintain His love, erases fear of rejection, frees us to accept and value others in the same way God accepts and values us, unconditionally and with no strings attached, and enables us to minister without restraint.

Joy

Joy gives us a feeling of blessedness, happiness, and gladness; an internal sense of delight and jubilation. David said,

"Thou hast put gladness in my heart" (Ps. 4:7). Our joy isn't a superficial ecstasy that is contingent on external circumstances, but it is grounded in God. God never changes, so if He is the source of our elation, we can always be joyous. Even in the midst of problems and sorrow, we can praise God.

This feeling of joy is not of ourselves; it is Christ's joy. When Jesus told His disciples about the Holy Spirit He said, "These things I have spoken to you that My joy may be in you and that your joy may be made full" (John 15:11). The joy of the Lord is in us. It is released when we believe and act on the things He has communicated to us. It is a full joy—controlling, total, consuming. When others see that, regardless of our circumstances, we can rejoice and be happy in God, they are drawn to us and we are able to comfort them and administer joy to their lives.

Longsuffering

Longsuffering gives us a feeling of patience. It holds on under stress or trial, never striking back, even in the face of provocation or when retaliation would seem to be justified. It is full of mercy and hope.

As with all the fruit of the Spirit, longsuffering is an attribute of God. He is longsuffering toward us (Rom. 9:22). God endures our imperfections and mistakes when He could, and should, retaliate. He could unleash His power against us, but instead implants it within us in the person of the Holy Spirit. When we are Spirit-filled, we will be merciful; we won't try to get back at others or give them what we think they deserve. We will patiently tolerate their imperfections.

The fruit of longsuffering is the quality that keeps us from losing heart and giving up. "Let us not lose heart in doing good, for in due time, we shall reap if we do not grow weary" (Gal. 6:9). We have to be patient and not grow weary of waiting on God's timing. When we are longsuffering, we feel hopeful because we know that ultimately God will have His way.

Endurance is another aspect of patience. This enables us to be patient with others and to wait upon the Lord to do His work in their lives. We don't have to push or try to hurry things along in the flesh but are willing to wait for God to move when and how He chooses.

Peace

The fruit of peace gives us a feeling of tranquility, even in the midst of strife or disagreement. The Spirit sets us at peace with God and ourselves so we can also be at peace with others, even our enemies. "When a man's ways are pleasing to the LORD, he makes even his enemies live at peace with him" (Prov. 16:7). This inner harmony of soul eliminates the need to be defensive or fight to maintain our territory.

The apostle Peter, who, until he was captivated by the Spirit, was a very explosive, easily agitated person, beautifully defined the fruit of peace. He said it is "spiritual peace to be realized in and through Christ, freedom from fears, agitating passions and moral conflicts" (1 Peter 1:2 AMPLIFIED). First, Peter established that spiritual peace comes only through Christ. Apart from Him, there is no freedom from turmoil. If we do not have Him we are forced to rely on our own devices to maintain relationships and protect ourselves from harm. True peace is freedom from the things that debilitate us and bring conflict into our lives—freedom from fears. We have already seen that fear is negated when we rest in God's perfect love. We feel peaceful, regardless of what happens, because we are in Christ. He is our security, our Protector, our Savior. Even when we are most vulnerable, when we are asleep and totally at the mercy of our environment, God's Word promises we have nothing to fear.

The peace Peter described also is freedom from agitating passions—emotions that stir us up and ultimately cause us to sin. We are at peace with ourselves when the Spirit produces this fruit in our lives. We are subject to His leading and not our own fleshly desires. Agitation is replaced with a feeling of harmony and oneness with God.

Peter said spiritual peace is freedom from moral conflicts. When we know God's Word and are filled with the Spirit, we feel no conflict over what is clearly right or wrong. Many basic moral issues which cause stress for so many people are not bothersome to Christians because God has already set standards for us to follow. I don't have to wonder whether I should keep the lost wallet I found on the street or turn it back to the owner, contents intact. My unmarried daughter doesn't have to decide whether or not she should have an affair with a married man. My teenage son doesn't need to debate the pros and cons of cheating on a test. My husband doesn't waste energy or emotion trying to figure out how to pad his expense account without getting caught. Conflict arises when we choose not to heed such basic biblical ethics.

The fruit of peace eases stress and strife, creating a sense of well being and a feeling of unity with God and others.

Goodness and Gentleness

The fruit of goodness is upright behavior coupled with kindness and it generates feelings of usefulness. Frequently we refer to a person of moral integrity, who is kind and helpful to others, as a *good* person. A good person is other-centered rather than self-oriented, and when the filling of the Spirit produces this fruit in our lives, we have a sense of satisfaction because God uses us in positive constructive ways to contribute to the welfare and happiness of others.

I've coupled goodness with gentleness because the two are so closely related. Goodness produces feelings of kindness. Gentleness (which is almost a lost commodity in today's impersonal me-centered world) is gracious compassion; a feeling of tenderhearted empathy. Harshness and abrasiveness are the opposite of gentleness. Gentleness is actually goodness in action and manifests itself in many ways; the tone of our voices, a smile or hug, the actual words we speak and our response to the pain and needs of others. Gentleness is compassionate caring.

Frequently we read in the Gospels that the Lord had compassion toward people. He healed the lame and sick because He hurt for them (Matt. 14:14). Moved by gentle compassion, He touched the untouchables, the outcasts who were scorned and neglected by society (Mark 1:40–42). Jesus' heart stirred in tender response to lost souls and those with fumbling faith. "Seeing the multitudes, He felt compassion for them, because they were distressed and downcast like sheep without a shepherd" (Matt. 9:36).

Jesus multiplied the loaves and fishes because He was compassionately concerned for the empty bellies and physical well being of the men, women, and children who had been following Him around the countryside. Sensing their need, Jesus summoned to Himself His disciples and said, "I feel compassion for the multitude because they have remained with Me now for three days and have had nothing to eat; and I do not wish to send them away hungry, lest they faint on the way" (Matt. 15:32).

Out of gentle compassion, the Lord suffered with those who were brokenhearted because of grief and loss and was always especially kind and gentle toward women; supersensitive to our physical and emotional needs. Luke 7:11–15, the story of the widow of Nain, is a beautiful illustration of how the fruits of gentleness and goodness were manifested by our Lord. The woman didn't ask Christ to resurrect her son. She was so devastated by her grief that she probably didn't even notice Him. But He noticed her and immediately was filled with compassion. I've heard several sermons explaining that Jesus performed miracles primarily to prove that He was God. I disagree. Jesus performed miracles *because* of who He was: the good, kind, gentle, compassionate Son of Man. He changed the water into wine, fed the multitudes, healed the blind, and raised the dead because He cared. He brought the son of the widow of Nain back to life not to establish His credentials, but so the woman wouldn't have to be alone without husband and child.

Jesus was a sympathetic person. He pitied and felt sorry for people, but He was also empathetic. He was able to experience someone else's feelings as if they were His own. Empathy is intrinsic to the fruits of gentleness and goodness. Empathy is the ability to put yourself in the other person's shoes, to accept and understand how another feels, whether or not you agree with him or her. When we identify with others in this way, we can minister to and uphold them without being judgmental, condemning, or harsh and without compromising our beliefs.

Christ empathized with the woman caught in adultery. He understood how humiliated, angry, and frightened she must have been. He defended her against the angry mob, even though their accusations were true and even though He personally abhorred adultery. He didn't sidestep the truth. The Lord clearly let her know that what she had done was a sinful impeachment of God's law. He commanded her to "Go your way; from now on sin no more" (John 8:11).

Jesus did not condone the woman's actions, but neither did He condemn her as a person. He understood her immediate life-threatening problem and identified with her embarrassment, even though it was self-inflicted, and His tender compassion won her over; she fell at His feet and addressed Him as Lord. Truly, in all ways, Jesus was a gentle man.

As the Spirit manifests the fruits of goodness and gentleness in us, we will be more like Jesus—disposed to doing what blesses others, more concerned for their welfare and feelings than for our own. Judgmental attitudes will give way to compassionate understanding and harshness to kindness. We will truly become good Christians.

Faith

Faith is total trust in and complete loyalty to God. It results from personal surrender to God, apart from facts, and is grounded in a firm conviction that God is who the Bible says He is. Faith is the heart assurance given to us by the Spirit that the Lord will honor our trust. When we are Spirit-filled, the fruit of faith will be operational in our lives. When we doubt, our fidelity falters and we negate the filling. Jesus taught that doubt cripples faith. "Truly, I say to you, whoever says to this mountain, 'Be taken up and cast into the sea,' and *does not doubt in his heart,* but believes that what he says is going to happen, it shall be granted him" (Mark 11:23).

Doubt comes packaged in many different ways. I once heard the story of a man who claimed his great faith could move mountains. He told everyone that nothing would ever cause his faith to falter; he would never doubt God's power. One day, while he was fishing with a friend, he bragged about his great faith, "Why, I could even walk on water, just as Peter did."

"So, let's see you do it," his friend drawled.

The man put down his fishing pole, took off his shoes, rolled up his trousers, and sank when he stepped into the lake. He was astonished. "I—I don't know what happened. I was so sure I could walk on the water. I truly believed."

His friend laughed, "Then why'd you take off your shoes and roll up your pants?"

A little doubt can negate a lot of faith.

Jesus said that doubt springs from our hearts. The word heart is a reference to a person's total being: intellect, emotions, will, spirit, and body. It is grounded in the verb to breathe. Our heart gives us our get-up-and-go and we are propelled by whatever issues from our hearts, be it doubt or faith. Our hearts are the part of our being with which we love God. Jesus taught that the most important commandment of all is "You shall love the Lord your God with all your heart and with all your soul and with all your mind" (Matt 22:37). Faith involves trusting God totally, without any reservations. When we do, we feel confident because we know we can do all things through Christ's strength. When we manifest the fruit of faith, others learn to trust in and rely on us, and God uses our faith to minister to them, to nurture belief in them, as they sense the Spirit moving in our lives.

Meekness

Meekness is probably the most misunderstood Christian trait. In our culture we associate meekness with weakness, but the Bible teaches that Christ was meek and since He is also omnipotent, almighty God, we can assume that the two words are not synonymous. In his *Expository Dictionary of New Testament Words*, W. E. Vine noted that "the common assumption is that when a man is meek it is because he cannot help himself; but the Lord was meek because He had the infinite resources of God at His command" (vol. III, p. 56). Yet He never misused them. So, authentic meekness is a powerful restraint. In modern terminology, it is a "cool" temperament; the ability to keep one's wits and not be overcome by circumstances. The fruit of meekness produces a feeling of stability and subdued control.

Dr. Raymond Cramer, in his book *The Psychology of Jesus and Mental Health*, defines the meek as the easy going; those who take life calmly; persons who are not impetuous or given to frequent outbursts. The meek person is casual, collected and informal. He further observes that the meek will inherit the earth because "the person who has emotional stability and a calmness within the structure of his own personality, resulting from the ability to manage his conflicting stresses, will be around to pick up the pieces when everyone else has caved in" (pp. 79–80).

That's a description of how Christ lived. Because He was meek, He was always in perfect control and always kept the upper hand in any situation. Each time His earthly rivals, the Pharisees and Sadducees, tried to trap Him and make Him look foolish, He thwarted their efforts with peaceful resistance, usually by answering them, then walking away.

During most confrontations, Jesus was a man of few words. In any situation that harbored the potential for argument or violence, He exerted Himself through understatement. When the Pharisees and Herodians tried to trick Him into saying He wouldn't pay a poll-tax to Caesar because it would be placing him above God, Christ asked His accusers to show Him the coin used for the tax. "And they brought Him a denarius. And He said to them, 'Whose likeness and inscription is this?' They said to Him, "Caesar's.' Then He said to them, 'Then render to Caesar the things that are Caesar's; and to God the things that are God's.' And hearing this, they marveled, and leaving Him, they went away" (Matt. 22:19–22).

When His enemies accused Him of breaking the Law by healing a man on the Sabbath, He simply said, "Is it lawful on the Sabbath to do good or to do harm, to save a life or to kill?" (Mark 3:4). When the Pharisees accused Him and His disciples of breaking the Sabbath by picking and eating wheat from grainfields through which they were passing, He didn't scream and yell at them about how ridiculous their charges were. He reminded them that God is more concerned with the spirit than the letter of the Law.

His ultimate display of meekness was before His death. When He was hauled before the Sanhedrin and falsely accused, He said nothing at all (Matt. 26:62–63). His silence was meekness in the purest sense.

Jesus knew when to pursue a point and when to let it drop, when to restrain Himself in the face of provocation. When we are Spirit-filled, God is in control of our lives and we feel and act stably. We are able to stay calm and think clearly during crisis situations and minister to others during times of trial and stress. We possess the "coolness" of Christ.

Temperance

The fruit of temperance, which is self-control, is closely related to meekness and results in a feeling of control and the mastery of fleshly passions. It helps us handle temptation the right way. Self-control involves participating; it is the ability to do things without overdoing them. It involves abstinence; there *are* "thou shall nots" in God's code of ethics. But mostly, temperance involves moderation and balance. Paul described it this way: "All things are lawful for me, but not all things are profitable. All things are lawful for me but I will not be mastered by any" (1 Cor. 6:12). Anything that masters or controls us is sin because it usurps the place of the Master and the role of the Spirit.

Not everyone has to exert self-control in the same areas. For example, liquor is not a temperance issue with me. I thoroughly dislike the taste and smell of alcohol, so I don't drink—not because I'm exerting self-control, but because I'm not the least bit tempted by it. But set a piece of pecan pie in front of me and a battle rages, because for most of my life I've been mastered by sugar. I have to use every ounce of my willpower to keep from eating sweets. A dessert binge is as sinful for me as a drinking spree is for someone who loves alcohol.

Lack of self-control saps the power of the Spirit in our lives. As we practice restraint in the face of temptation and moderation over consuming habits or undesirable, debilitating emotions, we will feel satisfaction and control, for the Spirit has full dominion in our hearts.

Serving with Power

I hope that searching out these truths about the Holy Spirit has helped you know Him better and appreciate His work in you. He is the source of spiritual power for all believers. He is able to do great, wonderful, exciting things through us when we are willing to defer to His rightful position. Let Him be your spiritual teacher. Trust Him to guide and direct your life ministry, as Priscilla did. Expect Him to communicate God's truth to you and awaken Christ's thoughts, words, will, and presence within you. Be filled to overflowing with Him so He can manifest His magnificence, empower your service, and help you practice the Priscilla Principle.

FIVE

God's Gifts: Serving With Competence

"And since we have gifts that differ according to the grace given us, let each exercise them accordingly"

ROM. 12:6.

During the ten years I taught first and second grades in the Los Angeles city schools, I thoroughly enjoyed opening and sorting through the varied, and many times wierd, assortment of gifts the children gave me at Christmas and at the close of the school year. I wasn't interested in getting the gifts but in what they reflected. Each one embodied its own message. Some were practical: gloves, a chalk holder, book ends. Some were personal: jewelry, a wallet, a monogrammed desk pad. Some were extraordinary: a luscious sour cream banana cake with the recipe attached, two tickets to a concert at the Hollywood Bowl. Some were humorous: an anonymous Christmas card signed "You're the meanest teacher I ever had. Happy holidays," and a box of chocolates with three of the dark brown, corrugated wrappers glaringly empty. Others were poignant: a used tube of lipstick which a borderline retarded and physically abused boy had stolen from his mother's purse and wrapped in a dirty facial tissue; a half-empty bottle of cheap perfume from the class terror.

Those gifts were a reflection of the thoughtfulness of the children and their parents and they told me much about our student-teacher relationships. Despite their imperfections, most of them were given in love. They were a way for the boys and girls and their parents to say "We care."

The Nature of God's Gifts

God has given us gifts that are a reflection of His thoughtfulness toward us and are representative of our Parent-child relationship. Like the gifts I received from my students, they are practical, personal, extraordinary, and poignant. God's gifts are love gifts. And, like all true gifts, they are free. Unlike the presents the children gave me, God's gifts are good and perfect, ideally suited to the needs of the receiver and totally without flaws. "Every good thing bestowed and every perfect gift is from above" (James 1:17).

The greatest gift of all is Jesus Christ. "The free gift of God is eternal life through Jesus Christ our Lord" (Rom. 6:23). The most amazing truth in all of Scripture is that God gave sinful, unregenerate humans the gift of His Son because He loved them so much. His purpose in sending Christ was to save us from our sin, but His motivation was love: "God so loved the world, that He gave His only begotten Son, that whoever believes in Him should not perish but have eternal life. For God did not send the Son into the world to judge the world, but that the world should be saved through Him" (John 3:16–17).

As an extension of the gift of His Son, the Father sends the Holy Spirit to all believers. We have already seen that the

Spirit seals our salvation and that He is a supernatural power source who produces fruit in our lives and gives us the strength and vitality to minister. To help us use that power, God also gifts us, through the indwelling presence of His Spirit, to prepare, capacitate, direct, and help us develop competency in our life ministries.

Gracious Giftedness

God gifts us in two ways: through our natural, inborn human traits and abilities and through the spiritual gifts He bestows on us at the moment of salvation. Natural talents are the inherited, genetic characteristics God fashions within each person. These include things such as musical and mathematical ability, the physical dexterity and strength that makes good athletes, a knack for organizing, or leadership and management ability. These are all part of the human condition—our old nature—and all people possess them.

Spiritual gifts are a by-product of redemption, a part of our new spiritual nature, and are not merely an amplification of our human, natural abilities. Although there is a difference between spiritual gifts and natural abilities, there is a definite intermingling. Our natural talents and spiritual gifts are complementary to one another, each undergirds and enhances the other, and they work in conjunction with each other. I call this fusing between our human and spiritual traits *giftedness*.

The Spirit may choose to gift and use us in the area of our natural abilities, or He may not. For example, before she came to Christ, my friend Shirley was disorganized and scatterbrained. She was the homemaker's version of the absentminded professor. After she became a Christian, she gradually grew into an extremely competent administrator and has developed a great deal of common sense. For several years she has been helping other women organize their homes and time. She would actually go into their houses, help them rearrange closets and cupboards, set up duty schedules, and set goals. Now she is an administrative assistant to a well-known color consultant and has a stimulating new career, as well as an ability to make many women build up their self-esteem. I believe this happened because, when she was saved, God spiritually gifted Shirley in the area of administration, a sphere in which she had no natural ability.

I know several Christians who are successful, trained secular educators who have absolutely no desire to use those skills in the body of Christ. At thirty-two, Vonnie has a Ph.D. in education and is an outstanding junior-high English and history teacher. The superintendent of the Sunday school at her church can't understand why she doesn't want to teach in the junior-high department on Sunday mornings. Instead, Vonnie has an overwhelming burden for missions and for reaching out to others in the love of Christ. Her home always is open to strangers and someday she hopes to open a center in her neighborhood to provide food, shelter, and counseling for people who are unemployed or homeless. She spends a lot of her time working with the Red Cross. In the spiritual realm I think she has the gifts of hospitality and mercy. She definitely does not have the spiritual gift of teaching.

I, on the other hand, do. God chose to gift me in accord with my natural talents. I was trained as a secular teacher and administrator and have always been a goal-oriented, organized person. In my case, the Lord decided to extend those human traits into the spiritual realm. Priscilla apparently was gifted in teaching, administration, and hospitality. And, as we have seen, she utilized her abilities to the fullest to further the cause of Christ. Her competency in ministry was enhanced by her giftedness.

Regardless of how God chooses to structure our giftedness, what's important is that we use both our natural talents and spiritual gifts for His glory. "As each one has received a special gift, employ it in serving one another, as good stewards of the manifold grace of God . . . that in all things God may be glorified" (1 Peter 4:10–11).

The Gifts

Before we can properly employ our spiritual gifts, we need to know what they are. Dozens of gifts are mentioned in Scripture: healing, miracles, tongues and interpretation of tongues, craftsmanship, music, hospitality, and evangelism, to name a few. Some gifts are not accepted as valid today by all churches, so I will focus on the ones that most members of the body accept as operational in our time. Although each Christian receives his or her special set of gifts, every believer is expected to exercise all of the gifts in a general sense, because they are characteristics of the family of God. You may not have the gift of helps but that doesn't mean you can turn your back on someone who needs assistance. You may not have the gift of teaching but that doesn't mean you shouldn't study the Word and share God's truth with others. So, as you study the meaning of some of the gifts, you should learn about your overall obligations in the body, as well as be able to identify your own special areas of giftedness.

Wisdom

Wisdom is the ability to apply God's truth to everyday situations in a practical way and to use knowledge correctly. A person who has this gift is able to come up with reasonable, moral solutions to seemingly unsolvable dilemmas. Such a person's common sense and understanding of motives and consequences supersede human ability.

King Solomon had this gift. He exercised it when two prosperation because my husband has the gift of wisdom

titutes, who shared the same living quarters and had both borne sons, came to him and asked him to make a monumental decision. One of the women claimed the other had rolled onto her infant during the night and accidentally suffocated it, then switched the babies, taking the live one as her own and giving the dead baby to the plaintiff. The defendant accused her housemate of the same offense.

They argued back and forth, each trying to convince the king that she was telling the truth. It seemed as if any decision Solomon could make would be a guess. What if he gave the baby to the wrong woman? How could justice be served? The king said, "Get me a sword . . . Divide the living child in two, and give half to one and half to the other" (1 Kings 3:24–25).

One thing is certain; King Solomon understood mother love. The moment he threatened to have the child killed, the real mother protested. She preferred her child brought up by the other woman than dead. The mother of the dead child wanted to have the live baby killed—then she would not be alone in her grief.

Solomon immediately had the positive proof he wanted; he had identified the real mother. And "when all Israel heard of the judgment which the king had handed down, they feared the king, for they saw that the wisdom of God was in him to administer justice" (v. 28).

Wisdom is an awe-inspiring gift, especially in a world where so many people act with such impetuous irrationality. I've been blessed to see this gift in operation because my husband has the gift of wisdom. He has an uncanny ability to "read" people and to know when to speak and when to keep silent, when to pursue an issue and when to back off. He comes up with logical, workable, uncomplicated solutions to seemingly insurmountable problems. He also has a great deal of insight and the ability to weigh consequences and determine outcomes before their time.

All Christians are supposed to seek after wisdom. We have no way of knowing whether or not Priscilla had this gift, but we saw how she exercised wisdom when she approached and corrected the learned Apollos.

The Book of Proverbs is filled with injunctions urging us to activate God's wisdom in our lives. Proverbs 2:2 tells us to "make your ear attentive to wisdom." The proverbs teach that wisdom stems from fear of the Lord and living a righteous, obedient life. "The fear of the Lord is the beginning of wisdom" (Prov. 4:10). James counseled that we should petition the Father for a special outpouring of wisdom when we encounter trials and problems. "If any of you lacks wisdom, let him ask of God, who gives to all men generously and without reproach, and it will be given to him" (James 1:5). So, even without the special gift of wisdom, God's wisdom is available to us all and we should use it to increase competency in our life ministries.

Knowledge

The gift of knowledge is the ability to discern truth, through the impression of the Holy Spirit and the study of God's Word. It goes beyond accumulating facts and involves an innate awareness of truth. A person with this gift doesn't just learn truth but understands what it means and how to apply it. Many times teachers and pastors have this gift. They're the ones who are able to take a portion of Scripture and make it come alive, to pull ideas from it that you would not have thought of even after hours of study. They make the simple seem profound and clarify passages that are confusing and difficult to understand. They serve "dessert" as we feast on the meat of the Word.

With or without the gift of knowledge, all believers are supposed to know and be students of the Word. As with wisdom, knowledge is grounded in our relationship with God. "The fear of the LORD is the beginning of knowledge. . . . and the knowledge of the Holy One is understanding" (Prov. 1:7; 9:10). We are responsible to learn and live by God's truth and cannot claim ignorance because we haven't been gifted in knowledge. All of God's resources are available to us through the indwelling presence of the master Teacher. We must study the Scriptures and rely on the Holy Spirit to teach us truth.

Faith

All Christians have faith; it was given to us by the Father so we could believe in Christ and become His children. "For by grace you have been saved, through faith—*and that not of yourselves,* it is the gift of God" (Eph. 2:8). Not only are we saved by that God-initiated faith, but we live by it also: "We walk by faith, not by sight" (2 Cor. 5:7). Every believer must have faith in God and be faithful to Him because "whatever is not from faith is sin" (Rom. 14:23). And "Without faith it is impossible to please Him, for he who comes to God must believe that He is, and that He is a rewarder of those who earnestly seek him" (Heb. 11:6).

So, in a general sense, every Christian has the gift of faith, but the faith that is listed in Scripture as a spiritual gift goes beyond the normal boundaries of belief. It is the ability to trust God beyond what is probable or possible, to take Him at His word and act on it regardless of circumstances. To a person who has this gift, the super-natural moving of God is the most normal, expected thing in the world.

The pages of Scripture swell with accounts of people who had the gift of faith. Moses had this gift. How else could he have assembled approximately two and a half million men, women, and children overnight and lead them out of Egypt? Why else would he have extended his hand over the Red Sea or touched the rock with his staff without so much as a "But, Lord"?

Noah had the gift of faith—building that huge ark in the middle of the desert, when it had never rained. Abraham, the father of our faith, had the gift. When God tested him and told him to take his only son and offer him as a burnt offering, Abraham did exactly as he was told. When he and Isaac went up the appointed mountain, Abraham told his servants, "Stay here with the donkey, and I and the lad will go yonder and *we* will worship and return to you" (Gen. 22:5). He believed God would spare his son.

And, when Isaac noticed there wasn't a lamb for the sacrifice, Abraham said, "God will provide for Himself the lamb for the burnt offering" (v. 8). His faith didn't waver when he lifted the knife and poised it over his son's heart. He knew God, trusted God, believed God would fulfill the promise He had made to make a great nation through him and Isaac. He knew God would intervene, and He did.

Hannah had the gift of faith. She prayed for the Lord to give her a son even though she was barren, and, when he was born she named him Samuel, "Because I have asked Him of the LORD" (1 Sam. 1:20).

People who have the gift of faith always seem to turn immediately to God when any need arises. They are usually "prayer warriors," who not only receive many supernatural answers to their prayers but are undaunted when it seems that the Lord is turning a deaf ear to their requests. They never give up, never blame God, and sense His moving in every situation.

All Christians should have that kind of tenacity. Even though we may not be gifted in the area of faith, we should use our God-given faith to the uttermost limits and trust God completely.

Prophecy

The gift of prophecy is widely misunderstood by many to be a form of holy soothsaying. Before the Bible was completed, prophecy was foretelling. The Lord spoke warnings, judgments, and instruction through His prophets. When the written Word was completed, that kind of prophecy ceased. God closed the Book, so to speak. At the end of Revelation, John made the final, biblical prophecy: "I testify to everyone who hears the words of the prophecy of this book: if anyone adds to them, God shall add to him the plagues which are written in this book; and if anyone takes away from the words of the book of this prophecy, God shall take away his part from the tree of life and from the holy city, which are written in this book" (Rev. 22:18–19).

Once the writing of the Scriptures was finished, prophecy took on a different meaning. Now, it is not adding to God's Word or predicting the future, but expounding the Scriptures and prophesies and truths embodied in the Word of God. The gift of prophecy is the ability to take God's established, written revelation and explain it to others.

You probably see this gift in operation in the pulpit of your church since the nature of a pastor's calling seems to demand it. Some teachers also have this gift. Our modern-day prophets are those men and women who are able to articulate God's written Word, make Scripture clear, and relate it to life as Priscilla apparently did in the early church. Each of us, whether gifted in prophecy or not, should be adept enough in the Scriptures to explain God's Word clearly to others. In that sense, we are all prophets.

Teaching

The gifts of teaching and prophecy are closely related, yet there is a difference between them. Teaching is instructing others and maturing them in the faith, reproducing God's Word in others. It is a ministry of duplicating and discipleship. Paul admonished the young Timothy, "The things you have heard me say in the presence of many witnesses entrust to reliable men who will also be qualified to teach others" (2 Tim. 2:2). Generally speaking, a teacher goes into more depth and detail than a prophet.

The difference between the gifts of teaching and prophecy was clearly illustrated by Christ, who was both a prophet and teacher. Usually Christ taught by using parables: simple stories that were easy to understand—if the people hearing them had willing hearts and were seeking the truth. Most of His prophecies, however, were warnings about the times to come and about who He was and why He had come.

All Christians are to be teachers of sorts; we all learn from and are taught by one another. The gift of teaching goes beyond that normal passing on of knowledge. God gives it to "master teachers" who then analyze and interpret God's truth and communicate it clearly and systematically to others. People with the gift of teaching inspire others to become students of the Word and motivate them to learn on their own. In many ways, they parent God's children toward Christian maturity.

Administration

The gift of administration, which is sometimes referred to as *leadership* or *government*, is the ability to organize, lead people, and manage projects. Of course, all Christians are supposed to do things decently and in order and manage their lives in a godly fashion, but people with this gift automatically are able to initiate, coordinate, and oversee people and activities. They know how to delegate authority and assess and use the talents of others. Usually, people with this gift have a great deal of common sense.

Priscilla and Aquila obviously had this gift. They laid the foundation for several of the early churches, set up the basic structure, guided people into various ministries, and trained leaders. Generally, men and women who serve on church boards and committees have the gift of administration. People with this gift form the framework within which the body of Christ operates and attend to the business affairs of the church.

Exhortation

To exhort means *to arouse with words of advice, encouragement, and warning*. The gift of exhortation, which is sometimes referred to as the gift of counseling, is evidenced by the ability to comfort, help, console, encourage, counsel, and, sometimes, rebuke or correct, always using the authority of God's Word. A person who has this gift uses the Bible as a how-to textbook and does not speak from personal opinion. It is imperative that anyone who has the gift of exhortation be well versed in the Word, because God always counsels in accord with His Word.

Every Christian is, at one time or another, placed in a situation where he or she has to offer counsel. We are all to comfort and advise one another as the occasion arises. But a person with the gift of exhortation is a master counselor, someone automatically sought out for assistance and guidance, someone able to speak the truth in love without compromising biblical principles. Exhorters have directional ministries; they keep Christians from straying from the path of righteousness.

Discernment

The gift of discernment is the ability to separate the reality of God's presence and moving from satanic activity. We are all warned to be aware and wary of evil and the influence of demonic forces around us, to expect and watch for apostasy, but someone who is gifted with discernment has the ability to spot evil that supersedes any human awareness.

When Jesus told His disciples that He would have to go to Jerusalem and suffer and be killed, Peter reacted as any normal, loving, concerned friend would have. He cried, "God forbid it, Lord! This shall never happen to you!" (Matt. 16:22).

Christ immediately knew that Peter's outburst wasn't motivated by love but that the devil was trying to weaken His resolve through the words of a dear, beloved friend. The Lord turned to Peter and said "Get behind me, Satan! You are a stumbling block to Me; for you are not setting your mind on God's interests, but man's" (v. 23). Because the Son of Man had the gift of discernment, He was able to see that what looked like godly concern was actually a satanic ploy.

A similar situation occurred in the Acts of the Apostles, when Paul and Silas encountered the demon-possessed slave girl. For days she followed them around the city of Philippi crying out, "These men are bondservants of the Most High God who are proclaiming to you the way of salvation" (16:17). What she said was true. To all outward appearances, she seemed to be trying to convince people that Paul and Silas were authentic followers of the Lord. Nevertheless, Paul became greatly annoyed, turned around, and said to the spirit, "I command you in the name of Jesus Christ to come out of her!" (v. 18). And it immediately did. Paul discerned the presence of an evil spirit in the girl. He knew that she was a fortune teller and that her fanatic testimony, though true, was not a validation of their faith but a demonic harrassment that could be detrimental to their mission.

People who have the gift of discernment are able to detect the subtlety of sin, even when it comes wrapped in a cloak of apparent righteousness. They do not, however, see evil all of the time, everywhere they turn. If they did, the gift would be a curse instead of a blessing. People who have this gift say that God activates it for His purposes whenever He chooses. Many of them say they have an internal reaction to a person or situation, which they describe as a "warring of the spirits." The Holy Spirit within them reacts violently to the presence of evil in the other person. This is not a moral judgment or condemnation, nor something they think through on the basis of fact, but a physical and emotional response of the Holy Spirit to evil.

This gift serves as a protection to the body and frustrates Satan's efforts at infiltrating the church or destroying the personal witness of believers. Even those of us who do not have the gift are to test the spirits and alert ourselves to the wiles of the Devil.

Giving

In our materialistic society the gift of giving stands out like a radiant gem in stark contrast to greed. People who have this gift have a compulsion to seek out needs and give of their time and possessions. They let the Holy Spirit have full charge over their property and time. This gift was evidenced in the Philippian church. When Paul was on a missionary journey, they evidently sent him money. He commended them for their thoughtfulness, noting that "no church shared with me in the matter of giving and receiving but you alone for even in Thessalonica you sent a gift more than once for my needs" (Phil. 4:15–16).

When Jesus saw the poor widow giving her offering, He took note of the selfless spirit that accompanied this gift. He said, "Truly, I say to you, this poor widow put in more than all the contributors to the treasury; for they all put in out of their surplus but she, out of her poverty, put in all she owned, all she had to live on" (Mark 12:43–44).

All Christians should be generous and cheerful in their giving to one another and the work of the Lord. "Let each one do just as he has purposed in his heart; not grudgingly or under compulsion; for God loves a cheerful giver" (2 Cor. 9:7). Even when we give with pure motives, most of us plan how much time we'll expend or how much money we'll drop in the offering plate. We plan and ration our giving. But people with the gift of giving can't help but give. Many times they go without to supply to others. They don't think about what they're contributing but about what others are receiving. I don't mean to imply that people with plenty don't have this gift. Some do, but rather than amassing fortunes through investments or doing all of the things most of us would do if we could afford to, they give their surplus and spend their time bringing pleasure and joy to others. They lay up treasures in heaven when they could be storing up fortunes on earth.

I know a wealthy couple who every year anonymously give a luxury Caribbean cruise to some couple in their church who would never be able to afford it on their own. I know a well-to-do doctor's widow who continues her husband's healing ministry by secretly paying thousands of dollars of hospital bills for parishioners and spending every spare moment in Christian service. She hunts for ways to give away her time and money. That kind of spirit epitomizes the gift of giving.

Helps

People with the gift of giving are the "suppliers" in the body of Christ. People with the gift of helps are the "servers."

We are all to serve the Lord and one another, but people with the gift of helps have a compulsion to offer practical assistance wherever and whenever it is needed. When I was a little girl my mother belonged to the Willing Workers Circle at our church. Those women were always making clothes or collecting food for the needy. At the church they did extra cleaning that the custodian didn't handle. They prepared the church dinners every Wednesday night and were always the first ones on the scene when an emergency arose.

People with the gift of helps truly are willing workers. Priscilla's ministry was probably undergirded by people with this gift, or her ministry would not have been as far-reaching and effective as it was. Those gifted with helps are "always there," ready to lend a hand. Often, they are behind the scenes, receiving little attention or acclaim. Their work usually goes unnoticed until, on some rare occasion, something doesn't get done. Their practical ministries keep the body running smoothly.

Mercy

Mercy is a combination of empathy, sympathy, compassion, and tough love. Whereas people with the gift of helps reach out with their hands, people with the gift of mercy reach out with their hearts. All of us are to be merciful and to empathize with and bear one another's burdens, but people with the gift of mercy possess a sensitivity of spirit that enables them to identify and agonize with the pain and despair of others. They literally suffer with those whom the majority ignores—the poor, handicapped, retarded, sick, aged, abused, depressed, and mentally ill. They are the burden-bearers in the body, the hand-holders who cry with those who grieve and suffer alongside the afflicted. People who have this gift say they actually can feel someone else's pain as if it were their own; they actually hurt with that person. They help meet the emotional needs within the church.

By learning a bit about these gifts and their purposes, I hope you've been able to define more clearly your role and understand how you and your brothers and sisters in Christ use your giftedness to minister to one another, both within the body and in the world. Since gifts are so vital to life ministry, we need to learn as much about them as possible. Understanding what they are is not sufficient; we need to be aware of how they operate.

The Gift Principles

Christians today hear and talk a lot about spiritual gifts, but despite all of the conversation and instruction, there seems to be a great deal of confusion surrounding this crucial topic. We know the gifts exist, have some idea as to what they are, but don't know how to use them properly. The identical problem existed in the early church. The believers at Corinth were so confused about spiritual gifts and misusing them so badly, Paul found it necessary to admonish and teach them principles about using the gifts. He said, "Now, concerning spiritual gifts, brethren, I would not have you ignorant" (1 Cor. 12:1). We, like our spiritual ancestors, must learn some basic principles about the operation of spiritual gifts so we can minister with enlightened awareness.

Gifts Are Genderless

The first principle concerning spiritual gifts is: There are no male or female gifts. God disperses the gifts according to His sovereign will. Throughout the context of Scripture men and women were endowed with identical gifts. For example, Priscilla and Paul both appear to have had the gifts of teaching, prophecy, and administration. Since there are no male or female gifts, it follows that sexual restriction in ministry is negated on the basis of giftedness, yet many churches act as if gifts are sexually bestowed. Stereotypically, men are assumed to have gifts such as knowledge, administration, and prophecy, so they can fulfill their roles as rulers in the body of Christ, while women are thought to have the more "feminine," or service-related, gifts of helps, mercy, and faith, so they can support the men.

Most churches accept that both men and women can have the gift of teaching, but a large percentage impose restrictions on the way women use that gift. Some won't let women teach men, including junior-high boys, yet all seem willing to let women teach children, the most pliable and easily influenced group in any church.

When sexual restrictions are placed on the employment of gifts, the entire community of believers is suppressed. In *Woman Be Free* Patricia Gundry says, "The church as a body is denied internal freedom under which it flourishes best. It is denied the benefits from the spiritual and intellectual gifts of half its membership when those gifts conflict with its stereotyped views of women possessing them. Every woman with something 'unacceptable' to offer suffers, and those to whom she would minister lose her help. . . . What body can work to full potential if half its members are bound with ropes and blinders so that full motion and vision are impossible. The body, which is the church, has bound its women in this way" (pp. 12, 33), and one reason this oppression exists is because Christian men and women do not believe God doesn't have sexual double standards. Only the Holy Spirit, who guides us into all truth, including truth about where, how, and whom we are to serve, can impose restrictions. Giftedness, coupled with the leading of the Spirit in each individual's life, is the basis for ministry and is intrinsic to the Priscilla Principle.

Defining Gifts

A second gift principle is: You can possess and be using your gifts without knowing or defining them. If people are always coming to you for advice and you have a talent for helping them search out answers to their problems, you have the gift of exhortation, whether you know it or not. If you've been teaching three-year-olds in Sunday school for five years, love every minute of it, and can't imagine wanting to do anything else, you have the spiritual gift of teaching. Although it isn't necessary to identify our gifts before we use them, we should be aware of what they are. It is better to serve from knowledge than in ignorance.

In some ways, you "grow" into a knowledge of what your gifts are. Paul taught that the body of Christ operates on the same principle as our physical bodies. Both grow and mature. When a child is born, he or she receives certain abilities that are not evident at birth but which surface over a period of time. My son, Brian, has a great deal of musical ability. He loved listening to music from the time he was a baby. Even when he was in preschool his teachers frequently remarked about how much rhythm he had. When he was ten he started taking piano lessons and, in the last two years, has become quite adept on the trumpet. Now he wants to take another year of piano, then learn to play the saxophone, drums (maybe I can talk him out of that one), and guitar. He also writes music.

When Brian was two he didn't say, "Someday I'm going to play the trumpet." At thirteen, he still doesn't know what the final outcome of his musical pursuit will be, but he has matured to the point where he knows he is talented in that area and wants to use and develop his ability.

When we are born, through faith in Christ, into the family of God, we receive certain gifts that are not evident but which surface, as we mature. We grow into them as we walk with the Master and follow the leading of the Spirit.

Identifying one's own gifts is not difficult. First, examine what you're good at, what you want to do, and enjoy doing. God enables us in areas in which He calls. He creates within us a desire to serve in our gifted areas. We should have fun and take pleasure in our ministries. I'm not implying there won't be problems and heartaches, but, in the long run, joy and satisfaction will overshadow them.

Second, use trial and error as a process of discovery. The Lord doesn't strike us dead for exploring possibilities. He rewards pure motives and honest efforts. Evaluate whether or not your service is generating godly results and producing fruit.

Third, take cues from other Christians. Many times God uses our brothers and sisters in Christ to reveal our gifts to us. When people who know and love the Lord say things like "You know, you're really very good at . . ." or "Have you ever thought about doing . . . ?" listen! Sometimes they see capabilities we've overlooked.

Fourth, pray. Ask God to help you discern what your gifts are. Ask Him to reveal to you what your gifts are, and to help you develop them and use them properly.

Gifts Are God-Given

One of the reasons Christians have difficulty defining their gifts is because they try to tell God what gifts He should give them instead of accepting the ones He's already bestowed. They overlook the third gift principle: God is the Source and Selector of the gifts. We may not ask the Lord to give us a certain gift (that's a mistake the believers in the Corinthian church were making), because "the one and the same Spirit works all these things, distributing to each one individually, *just as HE wills"* (1 Cor. 12:11). Our spiritual giftedness comes through the indwelling presence of the Holy Spirit, by the sovereign design of God, not through our seeking or asking. There is no way we could know which gifts we should have. God alone can determine that. He's the only One who knows how to fit us into the workings of the body, the One who is capable of deciding how He'll use us. "God has placed the members, each one of them, in the body, just as He desired" (1 Cor. 12:18). God selects and sends the gifts, we define and develop them.

Gifts Don't Make Us Spiritual

Some of the members of the church at Corinth had trouble being satisfied with the grace gifts God had assigned them. Instead, they sought after certain "showy," or foreground, gifts—those that called attention to the individual and seemed to indicate that he or she was more spiritual for having it. Paul sternly refuted the misconception that gifts make us spiritual. He explained that without the fruit of love, the gift of tongues is useless noise, the gift of giving is invalidated, and the gifts of prophecy, knowledge, and faith are rendered meaningless.

Yet today, many Christians are making the same mistake the Corinthian church made. We elevate people because of their gifts and equate spirituality with notoriety. We are as ignorant as our early counterparts about the fourth gift principle: Gifts are not a sign or guarantee of personal holiness. Gifts themselves are spiritual, but they do not make us spiritual. Further, our gifts do not validate our spirituality; our spirituality validates our gifts. An unyielded, disobedient Christian may possess enormous spiritual giftedness yet be totally carnal. Because humans look on the outward appearance rather than on the heart and because we are respecters of persons, we assume that the more gifted persons or those with "larger" ministries, are more spiritual or holy. That is not so! We are completely spiritual when we are controlled by the Spirit and totally carnal or unspiritual when we are operating in the flesh. Sin negates spirituality.

All Gifts Are Equal and Necessary

After Paul taught that giftedness is not synonymous with personal righteousness, he stressed that each of us should accept and appreciate the gifts God has given the others. He established the fifth gift principle: There is no hierarchy of gifts. All gifts are equally important and necessary, regardless of how showy or distinctive some may seem and how common, others. Paul sharply rebuked the Corinthian congregation for exhibiting such superficiality about gifts and for coveting what they erroneously believed were important, better gifts. His words should serve as a warning to us, not to get caught in the same mentality.

Repeatedly, Paul stressed that the church is one, unified body whose members perform varied but vital functions. "For even as the body is one and yet has many members, and all the members of the body, though they are many, are one body, so also is Christ. For by one Spirit we were all baptized into one body, whether Jews or Greeks, whether slaves or free, and we were all made to drink of one Spirit" (1 Cor. 12:12–13).

Paul pointed out, by comparing the body of Christ to the human body, how ridiculous it is for Christians to reject their God-given gifts just because they want different ones. He reasoned that a foot doesn't balk because it's a foot and not an arm, nor does an eye balk because it wants to be a hand. "If the whole body were an eye, where would the hearing be? If the whole were hearing, where would the sense of smell be? But now God has placed the members, each one of them, in the body, just as He desired. And if they were all one member, where would the body be?" (vv. 17–19).

Think about the human body. We respond to and pamper the external. We compliment people about their looks, tell them they have beautiful eyes, lovely hair, or a nice figure. We react to the showy parts. I doubt if you've ever been told what beautiful lungs or liver you have, yet it's easier to live without an eye or a leg than without a kidney or a stomach. Those vital, internal organs, which go unnoticed and are usually ignored until they break down, are just as necessary. "But God has so composed the body, giving more abundant honor to that member which lacked, that there should be no division in the body, but that the members should have the same care for one another" (vv. 24–25). God's distribution of gifts is on the same principles of harmony that He has shown in the human body. So whatever your gifts may be, they are equal with and as essential as all other spiritual gifts. We must accept, respect, and value the operation of every gift.

Gifts for Growth

Sometimes Christians are confused about why God gifted them. They act as if He did it as a personal favor. Actually, all of the gifts are referred to in Scripture as grace gifts, which means they are an undeserved, unearned outpouring of blessing. The Father sent them to equip us for service, not to make us look good. The gifts are given "for the equipping of the saints for the work of service, to the building up of the body of Christ" (Eph. 4:12). Gift principle number six defines the purpose of gifts: Gifts are essential for the growth and operation of the body of Christ. We are not gifted for self-edification or exaltation, but "to each one is given the manifestation of the Spirit for the common good" (1 Cor. 12:7).

For example, I go to a Bible study class and am taught by

someone who has learned from someone else. I study, learn, and grow because numerous people ministered the gift of teaching. I pass on what I have learned through my speech and example or because I incorporate the content into what I teach or write in my books. Then someone I teach studies and learns and passes on his or her knowledge, and, as a result, the body of Christ grows and flourishes.

When Brian was young I could not have maintained my speaking ministry if I had not been undergirded by friends who had the gift of helps, who readily baby-sat and fixed meals for my family. My teaching ministry would fizzle were it not for people who have the gift of faith and pray diligently for me or for those who have the gift of exhortation and do follow-up counseling. I'd never be asked to teach or write a book were it not for men and women who have the gift of administration, who plan the projects in which I get involved. There is no way to overemphasize the interdependency of gifts. A healthy body needs all of its members. We supplement one another's lacks and enhance each other's strengths.

Use Your Gifts

Since all gifts are essential to the growth and welfare of the body, it stands to reason that growth is stunted and development retarded when Christians do not use their gifts. The seventh gift principle is: Gifts must be used. Paul exhorted the church at Rome to exercise their various gifts. "Since we have gifts that differ according to the grace given to us, let each exercise them accordingly" (Rom. 12:6). Just as physical exercise contributes to the health of our physical bodies, exercising spiritual gifts contributes to the health of the body of Christ. I have been exercising for several years and one thing I have learned is that you can't store stamina or flexibility. If I go more than a few days without doing my aerobics and stretching exercises, I get out of shape. One instructor told me that a week of inactivity will undo three months of conditioning.

Furthermore, I've found that if I skip a week of exercising, it's hard to start up again. I can come up with all kinds of plausible excuses for why I shouldn't go to the gym or take a walk after dinner. And if I neglect my regimen for too long, inches pile up on my frame and my body gets flabby and my joints get stiff.

The same thing happens in the body of Christ when some members do not exercise their gifts—the body deteriorates and weakens. Spiritual atrophy sets in because gifts are meant to be used. If we are not using our giftedness, we aren't just hurting ourselves but the whole church. Every Christian in the world can be harmed and rendered less effective by one person's neglect. "And if one member suffers, all the members suffer with it; if one member is honored, all the members rejoice with it" (v. 26). Paul prodded Timothy to use his gifts: "Do not neglect the spiritual gift within you . . . I remind you to kindle afresh the gift of God" (1 Tim. 4:14; 2 Tim. 1:6).

We too should heed Paul's words, as Priscilla obviously did. Her ministry is proof that she used her gifts to the utmost. She taught, organized the Lord's work, and reached out in love to her community.

Gifts Are Not Fruit

Some Christians falsely assume that spiritual gifts and fruit are synonymous. The eighth gift principle states: Gifts and fruit are not the same. Fruit is the identifying characteristic of a Christian, the righteous, outward manifestation of the presence and filling of the Holy Spirit in the life of a believer. Gifts are God-given capabilities that help us minister and serve. As we have seen, all Christians are gifted. Our gifts are selected and bestowed by God, as He wills. The Holy Spirit helps us minister competently by giving us gifts. Gifts also help us define our areas of service. The fact that I have the gift of teaching shows me one general way in which God wants me to minister.

But not all Christians produce fruit. Whereas our giftedness is an ever-present absolute, fruit-producing occurs only when we are filled with the Spirit and are surrendered to God's will. Whether or not we are using our gifts, they are always a part of us. I don't lose my teaching ability when I am not conducting a class. Our ability to produce fruit, however, varies, depending on whether or not we are submitted to the Spirit at any given moment. We can minister without being Spirit-filled, but we cannot manifest fruit unless we are controlled by Him. Ideally, fruit and gifts are interdependent. As the Holy Spirit produces His fruit in our lives, we use our giftedness in a manner that is pleasing to the Lord and receive personal blessing.

Counterfeited Gifts

The ninth gift principle explains that gifts can be and sometimes are counterfeited. Most commonly they are counterfeited in the flesh when a Christian humanly tries to perform without being Spirit-filled. This is easy to do if you are naturally adept in the same area as your gift. When I teach or lead a seminar it would be very easy for me to rely on my educational background and the techniques I've developed through the years. There have been times when I've done just that, and I doubt if anyone in the audience knew I wasn't filled with the Spirit, but I knew because I didn't have any peace or joy; I was fulfilling an obligation rather than serving the Lord.

Fortunately, ministering in the flesh doesn't thwart God's Word or plans; it simply negates blessing in the life of a believer. God uses His message, apart from the messenger, to accomplish His purpose.

Gifts can also be counterfeited by Satan. He tries to infiltrate the body by duplicating the gifted performance of believers. The fact that the devil would counterfeit the gifts illustrates their high value to God. Thieves counterfeit money, not newspaper. No one counterfeits something that isn't valuable. Satan doesn't have to fight to get the world. It already belongs to him. He wants the church, God's people. So, he intervenes in the area of gifts, creating jealousies, envy, false ministries, and erroneous interpretation of doctrine. Satan's counterfeiting is another good reason why we shouldn't judge anyone's spirituality on the basis of gifts. Rather, we should examine fruit. Second Corinthians 11:13–15 very clearly warns that spiritual counterfeiters, sometimes called apostates, will invade the body. These phonies are masters at subtle deceit. "For such men are false apostles, deceitful workers, disguising themselves as apostles of Christ. And no wonder, for even Satan disguises himself as an angel of light. Therefore, it is not surprising if his servants also disguise themselves as servants of righteousness" (2 Cor. 11:13–15).

For some unknown reason, we seem to expect these false teachers to walk into church with a big red "A," for apostate, hung around their necks. On the contrary, they will infiltrate as unobtrusively and kindly as possible and do whatever is necessary to preserve their anonymity. "There will also be false teachers among you who will secretly introduce destructive heresies" (2 Peter 2:1). The apostle John advised that we not believe every spirit, but test them "to see whether they are from God, because many false prophets have gone out into the world" (1 John 4:1).

We are unwise and naive to accept that a person is truly a Christian merely on the basis of gifts. We should "test" everyone for authenticity. Does each manifest the fruit of the Spirit, not just a superficial piousness? Do a person's actions and works meet God's requirements and standards for righteousness? Is he or she ministering gifts with love and concern, or dogmatically and demandingly? Do beliefs and message consistently match God's written *and* living Word? Does a person cause dissension and confusion in the body? We must be on the lookout for these counterfeiters.

You Are Gifted

The tenth gift principle says that every Christian has at least one spiritual gift. This seems so obvious and simple that it almost appears unnecessary to state, but through the years I have met Christians who were convinced that, when God handed out the gifts, He overlooked them. First Corinthians 7:7 clearly states that each [person] has his [or her] own gift from God, one in this manner and another in that. Every believer has been spiritually gifted. Peter said, "Each one has received a special gift" (1 Peter 4:10).

There are three major theological theories about how many gifts each Christian has. Some scholars believe each person has only one gift. They base their conclusion on Peter and Paul both refering to a *gift*—singular. However, theologians who support a plurality of gifts theory contend the one gift or special gift of which Peter and Paul spoke is a reference to the combination of gifts God gives each believer, which meld into one. They say that just as the singular word *fruit* describes a composite of godliness in the believer, so the word *gift* describes a composite of gifts.

The second theory is that every Christian has one predominant gift with others to amplify it, and the third concept is that gifts come in combinations. I adhere to the last one because, subjectively, that has been my experience. I know I have more than one spiritual gift and that all of them are equally as strong. Actually, it is this plurality of giftedness that makes each of our ministries different and unique. God individualizes our service by combining our inborn, natural talents with certain spiritual gifts. Since no two people are alike, no two ministries will ever be the same. None of us will duplicate what another does.

Paul taught that there are varieties of gifts and also varieties of ministries and effects. "Now there are varieties of gifts, but the same Spirit. And there are different kinds of ministries, but the same Lord. And there are varieties of effects, but the same God who works all things in all persons" (1 Cor. 12:4–6). Two people may have the same gift but they will use it differently and the results of their ministries will vary.

For example, Susie and I both have the gifts of teaching and administration. I love teaching large groups—the bigger the better. I prefer a group of a thousand to one of ten any day, so God has me teach seminars or speak at events where there are large audiences. I use my gift of administration primarily in organizing study materials and writing books. I do not like to serve on committees. I like to help initiate ideas then turn them over to others to implement.

Susie prefers one-on-one discipleship and gets stage fright if more than fifteen women show up at the Bible study she teaches in her home. She's a whiz at working on group projects and is always chairing or serving on some board. We have the same gifts, but very different ministries and results.

God's Gifts Are Directional

God uses the unique combination of our talents, spiritual gifts, and personalities to further His kingdom on earth and build up His body. But our God-bestowed giftedness is also the Lord's way of helping us define our ministries. The Spirit leads us to serve in areas where we are gifted. The final gift principle is that God's gifts are directional. We have already discussed that Christians are indwelt by and have the capacity to be controlled by the Holy Spirit. When we are filled, God is then able to reveal His perfect will to us. He does this by embedding it in our hearts then sovereignly structuring circumstances, by planting His desires for us in our souls then bringing them to fruition.

SIX

Spirit-Planted Desires

*"Delight yourself in the Lord, and He
will give you the desires of your heart.
Commit your way to the Lord; trust
also in Him, and He will do it"*

Ps. 37:4–5.

God wants us to live our lives as ministries. He empowers us through the indwelling of His Holy Spirit, draws others to us by producing fruit in us, helps us serve competently by giving us gifts, and structures our life ministries through what I call *Spirit-planted desires*. Learning what Spirit-planted desires are and how to identify and respond to them will revolutionize your life ministry.

We often misinterpret Psalm 37:4–5. We take the statement "He will give you the desires of your heart" to mean that God will give us anything we want—anything our little hearts desire. If that were true, we'd act like the fisherman and his wife in the old fable of the three wishes. We'd use God like a magic genie and end up with nothing because we're so foolish and selfish. Most of the time we don't know what we want or what's best for us. Actually, that verse is a conditional promise: If we delight, God will reveal His will to us.

Delighting in the Lord is the singular qualification for activating Spirit-planted desires. Delight is an old-fashioned word which isn't used much anymore. Think of what warms your heart and soothes your soul: balmy breezes, a bubbling brook, the sound of music, a technicolor sunset, an unexpected love gift of flowers, holding a new baby for the first time. We delight in things that are emotionally and physically pleasant, that tantalize the senses and stroke the emotions and that we enjoy doing.

Delighting in the Lord means taking pleasure in Him. It is grounded in obedient, righteous behavior. "Yield now and be at peace with Him; thereby good will come to you. Please receive instruction from His mouth, and establish His words in your heart. . . . For then you will delight in the Almighty, and lift up your face to God" (Job 22:21–22, 26).

Delighting is turning from self, and from seeking what we want, to God and worshiping Him in the fullness of our spirits. "If . . . you turn your foot from doing your own pleasure, desisting from your own ways, from seeking your own pleasure, and speaking your own word, then you will take delight in the Lord" (Isa. 58:13–14).

When you fulfill your part of the promise (by making the most of your love relationship with the Lord), then He fulfills His. He gives you the desires of your hearts. He makes His will your will, He causes you to want what He wants. He instills within your mind, emotions, and human awareness His specific, godly desires for you and reveals the things He has prepared for you to do. God leads through Spirit-planted desires; all we have to do is delight in Him then recognize and respond to them.

Identifying Spirit-Planted Desires

All Christians have Spirit-planted desires. I do, your pastor does, you do; but you may not recognize them as such, because they are things you so badly want to do, would enjoy doing, and would be good at. Unfortunately, many Christians assume, if that's the case, that those desires certainly couldn't be God's will. Spirit-planted desires may be things you've squelched in the past because you wanted so much to do them, or because they sounded so far out that you couldn't summon up the courage or faith to try them.

For some ridiculous reason, we think God is going to force us to do something we dislike. Intellectually we accept that God is a loving, merciful Father then we act as if He purposely plans ways to make our lives miserable. In Luke 11:11–13 Christ explained how ludicrous that misconception is. "Now suppose one of you fathers is asked by his son for a fish, he will not give him a snake instead of a fish, will he? Or if he is asked for an egg, he will not give him a scorpion, will he? If you then, being evil, know how to give good gifts to your children, how much more shall your heavenly Father give. . . ?"

Sometimes we miss God's best because we're expecting less or because we've predetermined how His will for us will come packaged.

I don't want any of you to miss God's best because you expect too little or because you ignore the obvious—those wonderful, holy dreams and ambitions the Holy Spirit has implanted in your heart.

Discerning the Direction

God works marvelous, magnificent wonders through people who follow their Spirit-planted desires. Leroy Larsen had a Spirit-planted desire to feed, clothe, and provide shelter for poverty-stricken families. The dream came to him during a time of adversity. Asthma had kept him out of work for over a year and he weighed ninety pounds, when he told God he would serve Him—whether or not he was healed. Within two weeks he gained thirty pounds and eventually started delivering food to the slums of Tijuana, Mexico. Now he and volunteers regularly take a school-bus load of groceries and clothes to the poor.

The *Los Angeles Times* (March 3, 1983) quotes him as saying, "'When you start ministering for Christ, He broadens your ministry.'"

Leroy Larsen and his family are no different from you or me. He's a man who loves the Lord and ministers his gifts in accord with his Spirit-planted desires.

Cindy also had a Spirit-planted desire. Several years ago, when I was teaching this concept at a retreat, she came up to me and shared that since she was five years old she had felt a Spirit-planted desire to be a professional singer. She'd sung in glee clubs, as a soloist with a combo during high school and college, and always with the church choir. "But," she confided almost guiltily, "that's never been enough. Deep down in my heart I've always wanted more: to be a star, to make records and sing for the whole world."

She admitted she thought her desire was selfish and sinful, so she had stuck to being a wife, mother, and soloist at the church. We discussed ways she could pursue a music career, starting with telling her husband of her dream. She followed that God-given desire and is now a well-known performer. She readily shares her faith and gives God the credit for her happiness and success.

I can personally testify that if I had tried to structure my life and career I would have failed miserably and never received the multitude of blessings God has poured out on me. I'd probably be a school principal and still be trying to sell the articles, stories, and books I write if God hadn't shown me His will through Spirit-planted desires. I know that when I accepted Christ at the age of eight, He planted and activated my desire to write. I was always writing something, but not until I started delighting in the Lord, some thirty years later, did my material sell. But during those intervening years He used every experience, every problem, every victory and defeat, every circumstance and person in my path to bring me to the point that I became a published author whose emphasis is writing Christian material. But writing wasn't the only career ministry God had planned for me.

I first got a glimmer of the concept of Spirit-planted desires when I turned my life back over to the Lord, after having been carnal so many years people didn't even know I was a Christian. One of the first things I did was go on a women's retreat at Forest Home Christian Conference Center, a lovely mountain resort that's nestled in a story-book setting in the San Bernardino Mountains.

Our pastor's wife, a bubbly, vivacious redhead who had a burning love for the Lord, a deep burden for lost souls, and the gift of teaching, conducted the first teaching session. As she stood behind the podium instructing hundreds of women, something very strange happened to me. No matter how hard I tried, I couldn't keep my mind on what she was saying, which was strange for me because I was so hungry for the Word that I devoured anything I heard, like a starving person would eat anything in sight. Instead of listening, I kept thinking, *Oh Lord, I would so much like to be doing what she's doing*. I wanted it so badly I could almost taste it. My first reaction was guilt! I remember thinking, *Why, Jo Berry, what is the matter with you? You've never been a jealous person and here you are envious of your own pastor's wife, who also happens to be one of your dearest friends.* I, like so many others, initially rejected my Spirit-planted desire as sin.

After a while I reasoned, *No, I am not envious or jealous of her. I don't want her to stop doing what she's doing or detract from or interfere with it in any way. I don't want to take her place; I just want to do what she's doing.*

From that moment on, that consuming, overwhelming,

burning desire churned in my heart. About six months later, opportunity knocked, although it came dressed differently than I'd envisioned. I was asked to be missionary chairperson of the church's women's fellowship group, which meant I was to handle all of the correspondence with the missionaries we supported and read their letters at our monthly meetings. I was to read right after the lunch and before the main speaker appeared—about the time when everyone took a short nap. I honestly admit I had very little interest in missions, but I thought something needed to be done to stir up interest and concern in that area. I went to the nominating committee and accepted the position—if, instead of reading all those long, drawn-out letters each month, I could feature a specific missionary, going into detail about his or her ministry and sharing prayer requests. I also asked if I could give a devotional to fire up a burden for missions. That was the start of my teaching-speaking career in the body of Christ. You'd be surprised how many mission-oriented devotionals a person can come up with if she wants to badly enough.

From then on it was easy going. I was asked to help teach a Bible study, then gradually speaking requests came my way. Eventually, I quit teaching school to devote my full energies to Brian and my speaking, teaching, and writing.

The Lord has indeed been gracious, as fourteen years after my first visit to Forest Home, I stood behind the same podium as had my pastor's wife, teaching hundreds of women. God added the perfect finishing touch by bringing me full circle, for in the exact place it began, He brought to full fruition the desire He had planted in my heart. I had delighted in the Lord and committed my way to Him; He had ingrained in me the desire and He brought it to pass. God's Word is always true. It never fails. His Spirit is always ready to lead if we will but follow, in faith.

But, I'm Married

When speaking at a recent conference, I was approached by a young woman. "Can I ask you an important question?" she began hesitantly. I always shudder a bit when someone starts a conversation that way because it usually means a heavy—one of those unanswerables such as, Why does God let babies die? Or is abortion acceptable if a woman has been raped?

We found a seat in the back corner of the auditorium, and she asked, "Does my husband have a right to tell me what my ministry should be?" She went on to explain that she knows she is gifted in a certain area and desires to use her talents in a music ministry, not so much at the church but in her home, giving free or inexpensive piano and voice lessons to children whose parents can't afford to pay for training. She also wants to let them use her piano for practice if they don't have one in their home.

Her husband, who is a deacon-elect, wants her to become involved in his ministry. At their church, if a deacon's wife doesn't consent to serve beside her husband, he is usually denied the position. She didn't want to be unsubmissive or unsupportive of his ministry but she had neither the desire, nor, she believed, the ability to assist him in the expected way. She would have had to attend monthly board meetings, hold quarterly dinners in their home, and pay a required number of sick calls each month. She was torn. What should she do?

I suggested that she first sit down with her husband and try to reach a compromise. Could she miss the board meetings and would he do all of the sick calls if she would prepare and host the quarterly dinners? Could she limit her inclusion in his ministry without being as involved as the church demanded? Second, I suggested that she needed to develop her own theology of ministry so that she can act on thought-out principles and beliefs rather than on emotions or guilt.

I don't know what happened in their situation. That's the problem with breezing through town to do a weekend seminar. I do know that it would not be right for that young woman to suppress the desires God is giving her or to quench the leading of the Spirit to satisfy her husband's and the church's wishes.

Doing the Desires

Right now, set this book aside and concentrate for a moment. Is there something you've always wanted to do but haven't? Something you've pushed to the back of your mind for months or years? A dream you've never shared with anyone because you feared it was too far-fetched or outlandish or drastically different to implement? Well, with God, far-fetched means limitless, outlandish means supernatural, and different means innovative. Start now to use your Spirit-planted desires and your giftedness to develop competency in your life ministry. Remember, all things are possible with God, who wants us to exercise the gifts He's bestowed.

SEVEN

New Beginnings

*"Therefore, if any man is in Christ, he
is a new creature; the old things passed
away; behold, new things have come!"*
2 COR. 5:17.

I love new things, don't you? New babies, with their teeny
fingers and sweet gurgling sounds. The fresh, crisp fabric of a
new dress. The wood and plaster smell of a new house. The
promise of growth embodied in a new friendship. I love the
feel of a new pencil in my hand. Stubs are so clumsy, but the
length of a new pencil helps the words flow onto the page.
Second Corinthians 5:17 is my favorite verse of Scripture.
How I treasure the promise of newness! Thank God when I
put my faith in Him, He didn't just put Band-Aids on the old
me; He didn't try to patch and paint my sinful soul. Instead,
He started over and re-created me; in Christ He made me a
new creature and gave me a fresh, new beginning.

That's what this book is about—new beginnings; starting
over; re-creating and redirecting ministries; experimenting
with ideas; adding depth and dimension; rejuvenating and
refreshing spirits; living like the new creatures we are. We've
been redeemed, gifted, and empowered; now we must react

and respond. We need to stop playing at "churchianity" and start practicing our Christianity.

"Have I been playing the game so long I no longer see how unreal and pretentious it is? Am I so into the game of appearances, correct platitudes and formal prayers that I cannot—will not—chance a *fresh, new beginning* of honest simplicity and humble obedience? O God! I need You to help me pull down the masks of my playlike self and help me crawl out from under the heavy burdens of rationalized righteousness. Forgive my sin, dear Father, and assure me that I don't need to play the game anymore to be accepted or to even be on the team" (Unknown).

It's time to stop playing the game. Time to freshen and restructure our approach to life ministry. Think new! Do things differently. Make necessary changes. Chance a fresh, new beginning, which is ours in Christ.

First Things First

Once we are motivated toward a cause, we may try to do too much too soon, which is one reason New Year's resolutions are so easily broken; it's impossible to change habits developed over a lifetime in one momentous gesture. So where do we begin? How do we start putting on the new self?

First you need to discard the old. Use the next few days to examine your attitudes. Try to discover what things you are doing "as to the Lord" and which ones you are doing in the flesh, because you have to. Before you tackle any task, whether grocery shopping, changing diapers, or taking a friend to lunch, pray and commit that activity to the Lord and ask Him to use it for His honor and glory and to bless your efforts.

As your attitude toward your tasks becomes more positive,

expand the scope of your service. Begin with some "cup of water" ministries. Offer to help others with little things. Lift a burden whenever possible. Remember, you don't have to move mountains; just eliminate a few ant hills. Keep your ears, eyes, and heart open. Start praying for people who cross your path: the UPS delivery person; the clerk at the grocery store; the teacher you've never met who is giving your brilliant child unfair, low grades. Minister with new vigor and enthusiasm to your husband, children, friends, and neighbors through your prayers and your availability.

Home Base

Making a new beginning involves identifying the different arenas for ministry God sets before us. Our ministries can be broken down into our spheres of influence, such as home, place of employment, recreation, and church. One basic, new approach involves establishing our homes as the base for our life ministries. Priscilla did. One could argue that she did so for cultural reasons, but I believe she realized the value of structuring her life ministry around her home. Most Christians use the church as the primary setting for service because they think of ministry as being church-related. We have seen, however, that that is not true. Ministry is life-related. Whether you're a homeowner or apartment-dweller, male or female, young or old, single or married, a parent or childless, the place that is the center of your life—your home—should also be the base of operation for your ministry.

There are several reasons for using your home as a base of ministry. The majority of people are most comfortable and at ease in their own homes, and therefore are more effective in what they do there than in what they do anywhere else. You can exert more control over what happens in your home than elsewhere. At work you're limited by the rules and regulations of an institution and by the ideas and opinions of a boss and coworkers. At church you're confined to doctrines, interpretations, and governmental structure, but home is your own territory. You set the boundaries, make the rules, decide what takes place. There you have unrestricted freedom of spirit and movement, and whoever walks through your doorways is, by the fact of his or her presence, acquiescing to your authority and right to say and do whatever you wish.

The other day Brian and his usual gang of five or six boys were playing basketball in our driveway. I was sitting in my office writing and I kept hearing someone say "Jesus Christ" in a defamatory way. I scurried outside, called "time out," and said, "I don't know which one of you is swearing, but I would like you to stop. We are Christians and we do not use the Lord's name that way, so while you're at our house, in our yard, I ask that you abide by our rules."

I exerted my prerogative to set behavior standards and the kids know thay have to abide by them.

But more important than personal freedom or control is the tremendous influence you can wield in your own home. When Jesus charged us to be His witnesses, He instructed us to begin in Jerusalem—the immediate vicinity. Symbolically, our Jerusalem is the place where we live—our homes. We have the greatest effect, positive or negative, on those closest to us. The closer you are to someone, the more intimate the relationship, the greater your sphere of influence over them. It makes sense, then, to concentrate on ministering to our families before we branch out into Judea and Samaria.

I've always believed that I could have a dynamic Christian witness in the world if I never stepped foot out of my front door. If I educate my children in the Word and send them out bathed in prayer, prepared to withstand evil, maintain godly standards, and share their faith, I am reaching dozens, even hundreds of young lives through my children. If I daily send a happy, contented husband out into the dog-eat-dog world and contribute to his well-being and equilibrium by providing a happy home and loving environment, I'm exerting influence over every person his life touches.

What I say and how I live my Christianity has a broader, deeper, more abiding impact on my husband and children than on people who read my books or attend the seminars and classes I teach. Certain ideas in this book may touch your heart. Concepts I teach may motivate or help some people who attend my classes, but that is insignificant compared to the influence I can have in the lives of my family and people who integrate their lives with mine in close friendship.

The committees or boards on which you serve, the services you render outside your home, the job you hold or career you pursue should never be as important to you as your home and family. You can always quit a board or committee, but you can never quit your family. Your employer can always replace you, but your family can't. The time and emotions you invest in the people closest to you bring the greatest return. A home ministry is the most valuable, enduring, influential there can be.

What's a Home To Be?

A home should be a stark contrast to the frantic, stress-filled world. Helen Lowrie Marshall wrote, "May the house you call home be a haven of rest, secure 'neath a roof of prayer." A Christian home should, by the very nature of its inhabitants and the Lord it honors, be a haven. It should be a shelter, a tranquil place where people can retreat from the chaos which bombards them in the outside world. It should be a refuge, a place where people feel safe emotionally as well as physically, where they are protected from the negative elements they face in the marketplace of life. It should be a place to establish roots.

The wife and mother of a household can do more than any other family member to create a peaceful, pleasant, loving atmosphere. She is a pacesetter. The essence of a Christian woman's home ministry is making her home a haven of rest.

Making Your Home a Haven

To turn your home into a peaceful, productive place of ministry, assess your present situation and establish what changes are needed. Then make a conscious, thoughtful effort to make your home a haven. Start by eliminating unnecessary stress and tension. Certainly all families have problems, and you have no choice but to face them as they occur, but handling them as calmly as possible without overreacting can soothe everyone's nerves. When many members in a family have hectic schedules and a multitude of varying responsibilities, minor upsets can seem like major tragedies. Far too often we make a mountain out of the proverbial molehill. Learn to roll with the punches. I sometimes ask myself, *What difference will this make five years from now?* Usually, the answer is none.

Many families let an excess of negative, outside influences filter into their homes. Conflicts from a job, time pressures resulting from too many involvements, worries caused by the weight of other people's problems, anxiety from making unfair and unnecessary demands on self and others, fears of all those horrible disasters that might happen but never do—all sap spiritual strength, waste emotional energy, and cause unnecessary stress. Eliminate as many of these destructive, negative elements as possible. There are a lot of problems and tensions that can, by choice, be avoided. They can't infiltrate unless you let them.

Scheduled Sanity

You can also make your home a haven of rest by controlling the way you and your family invest and manage time. The Bible teaches that God does not generate confusion, yet many Christian homes are chaotic rather than peaceful because the family doesn't operate on a schedule and individual members don't have assigned responsibilities. Scheduling breeds sanity and sanctity in a home. The confusion that results from lack of planning and discipline is very tiring and stressful in itself. No one can relax in a home with some constant irritating, minor upset or emergency caused by neglect or oversight. Every family needs a general time schedule: breakfast at seven, lunch at noon, dinner at six, homework done thirty minutes after getting home from school, bedtime at ten on school nights. A family also needs designated duties, so all members can contribute and so things get done in a reasonably calm fashion. Tommy dumps the trash; Jimmy mows the lawn; Susie folds the laundry; Mary sets the table. Once general boundaries are established, exceptions can be made on an "as needed" basis.

Overextending is another scheduling problem. Too many of us say *yes* to too many things and take on more than we can handle. The best way a family can spend their time is at home together. Opt for quality rather than quantity of outside involvement. Have *one* church-related ministry, *one* community service, and save time for yourself and the people you love. Spending too much time away from home automatically causes problems and disturbs the equilibrium of a home.

A Refuge of Love

A final way to make your home a haven of rest is to create a loving atmosphere. Make it a place where every family member is sheltered from evil, ensconced in righteousness, and unconditionally accepted and appreciated as a unique individual. In a loving atmosphere, each person, regardless of age, is allowed, even encouraged, to have and express varying moods and opinions. Members respect each other's rights and privacy. There is a family spirit because people support and affirm each other.

Intimacy is part of a loving atmosphere. Families should enjoy the emotional intimacy of friendship—close one-on-one relationships which include the sharing of confidences—and also a physical intimacy. Loving families touch, hug, kiss, back-slap, nudge, hold hands, bond themselves physically in different ways. They show their affection. Sometimes physical intimacy comes naturally. Sometimes it does not; it has to be learned. Close personal contact is a healing, fusing factor in a family and develops a sense of closeness and caring as nothing else can. A kiss on the cheek, an arm around the shoulder, or a pat on the back says "I love you" or "I understand" in a more meaningful and special way than mere words.

Once you've properly set the scene, you're ready to move on to phase two of the new beginning of your home ministry—to devote yourself to ministering to the people in your Jerusalem. As you think about making a fresh start in certain areas of your interpersonal relationships, remember this: Every rule of Christian conduct that applies in the church also applies in the home. If there are unsaved members in your family, you are a representation of Christ to them, a moment-by-moment sermon. The way you live your faith formulates their opinions about God. If your husband or son is a believer, he is also your brother in the Lord. If your daughter is a Christian, she is also your sister in Christ.

Your Wife Ministry

Within the arena of your home, you have ministries to many people: friends; neighbors; children; children's friends, parents, and teachers, and your husband. If you are married, your wife ministry is the most important of all and should take priority over the others. Too often, husbands and wives put the children first, and, as a result, once the children leave home, as they inevitably do, many married couples discover they have nothing in common; their entire relationship was grounded in the commonality of parenthood. These are the men and women who, after twenty-five or thirty years, get divorced.

In the magazine *Family Life Today*, Dr. Fitzhugh Dodson observed that "Your marriage comes first and your relationship with the children comes second. Too many families are child-centered rather than marriage-centered. This is not psychologically healthy. The marriage should maintain its own center of gravity, and the children will inevitably benefit from a happy, stable marriage" (Nov. 1982). Many experts, child psychologists, teachers, and social workers agree that happy, well-adjusted children are the by-product of a good, stable, loving marriage relationship between their parents. Dr. J. Allan Petersen has observed that children don't learn to love by being loved but by watching a mother and a father love each other. Someday, after the children are gone, there'll be just you and your husband, and, unless you center on and devote yourself to him and cultivate your love relationship throughout all the years of your marriage, you might well face some difficult problems when the nest finally empties.

Hundreds of books have been written and thousands of sermons preached and Bible lessons taught about the wife and husband ministry. Some spiritualize the relationship, others psychoanalyze it. I simply want to share three simple words that have helped me in my ministry as a wife.

The first is *fidelity*. Fidelity is a combination of trust, loyalty, and faithfulness. It's more than remaining physically faithful; it's mental allegiance and emotional commitment to your husband and your marriage. It is never saying or doing anything to detract from your husband's dignity or acting in a way that will shame or embarrass him. It's understanding that you are a reflection of his tastes and values and that he needs to be able to take pride in the kind of person you are. "An excellent wife is the crown of her husband, but she who shames him is rottenness in his bones" (Prov. 12:4).

Fidelity also is respecting your husband as a person and honoring his God-given position in your life. I've always found it most interesting that the Lord, through Paul's writing, directed husbands to love their wives but instructed wives to respect their husbands (Eph. 5:33). The Lord wants husbands to understand that their primary responsibility in a marriage is not to rule or subdue them, but *love* them, just as Christ loved the church. God wants wives to understand that above anything else, husbands need their respect, which is actually a mental attitude of acceptance and validity of a man's personhood. The Lord knew that respect, for a woman, precedes real love.

A wife should never do anything to detract from her husband's manhood. She needs to understand that she and her husband are one; whatever touches and affects him affects her as well. A faithful wife always puts her husband's best foot forward. She speaks well of him and doesn't publicly air his faults or their differences. She realizes that by being loyal to him, she is being true to herself. "She does him good, and not evil all the days of her life" (Prov. 31:12). And, because she has a faithful spirit, their interpersonal relationship is enriched: "The heart of her husband trusts in her and he will have no lack of gain" (Prov. 31:11). Her husband totally trusts her—her opinions, her actions, her responses, and her concern for him.

A second necessity in a productive wife ministry is *friendship*. Your busband isn't only your life partner, the father of your children, and your lover; he should be your best friend.

No doubt each of you, at one time in your life, has had a female best friend. Think for a minute about what that kind of close friendship involves. Best friends are confidants; they share secrets and their innermost feelings. You'd rather be with them than anyone else. You automatically rely on them for help and they are always available when there's a problem. Best friends hurt with you and stand up for you, even when you're wrong. They also understand your faults and weaknesses and are part of the chosen few who care enough to tell you the truth about yourself.

Your husband should be your best friend. In the overall scheme of a marriage, I believe this friendship factor is more important than romantic love. I have many good friends and several very close ones, but George is my best friend. He was the first person I wanted to tell when my first book was accepted for publication. He's the one to whom I immediately, instinctively turn when I'm hurt or upset. He's the person I most want to be with, do things with, talk to, and be near. I value his friendship as much as I value his love.

Friendship, like love, has to be cultivated. Try thinking of your husband as your best friend, and treat him as if he were. Spend more time just being together. Get to know him better. Enjoy being best friends with your husband.

The third vital ingredient in your wife ministry should be *fun*. Many Christian couples seem to have gotten so involved in learning about their roles, duties, and obligations that they labor at their marriages instead of taking pleasure and relaxing in them.

Being conscientious about your marriage is admirable, but don't be overly concerned about doing things according to the book or the experts' advice. Instead, establish your own standards for the relationship and concentrate on enjoying your life together. Think about your Spirit-planted desires in terms of your marriage. Devote more time to doing things you like and want to do for the sheer pleasure and enjoyment of experiencing it together. Focus on having fun and you'll discover an excitement and spontaneity in your marriage that you thought you'd lost.

Fidelity, friendship, and fun were undoubtedly factors in Priscilla and Aquila's marriage. We can only read between the lines to make our assumptions, but her faithfulness to their relationship is seen in the way she worked with and upheld her husband. They must have enjoyed being together and have worked well as a team, or they would never have accomplished all they did. Priscilla's life, in many ways, is reflective of an exemplary wife ministry.

Your Mother Ministry

Wife and mother ministries are closely related. Actually, the same factors contributing to success, happiness, and new life in a marriage do the same for parenting. A good parent-child relationship is grounded in fidelity; there is a mutual trust and respect of parent for child, as well as child for parent. It also embodies friendship, which involves spending time together, not trying to be a buddy or pal to them, but loving them enough to correct and discipline and to stand by them through any problems, even those of their own making. And a satisfactory parent-child relationship includes having fun with your children—enjoying them and getting to know them as people, apart from the fact that they're your offspring.

As with marriage, sometimes parents become so concerned with their roles and duties that they lose sight of their basic job: ministering to their children, bringing them up "in the training and instruction of the Lord" (Eph. 6:4). The King James Version uses the word *nurture*, which is the essence of a mother ministry. Nurturing is preparing your child for maturity and making certain you don't neglect or overdo one area in lieu of another. It's balancing your approach and developing every facet of your child: intellectual, physical, emotional, social, and spiritual. Nurturing is helping God grow your child from a fragile, incomplete soul into a strong, well-adjusted, independent, whole person.

Nurturing embraces several ideas. One is feeding and nourishing. A child's mind, body, and soul all need the proper nutrients: The brain must be fed clean, lovely, edifying thoughts; the body, good, healthful food; the soul, spiritual milk and meat from the Word of God. Each area of your child's life needs a balanced diet.

Nurturing also implies tending—sustaining a high quality of life and doing whatever is necessary to maintain physical, mental, and spiritual stamina. Just as unattended lawns and gardens go to weed then seed, untended children do not grow and flourish as those who are watched over and carefully supervised.

Children need to be unconditionally loved and accepted, because that's how God loves us. Love should never depend on their behavior and shouldn't have to be earned. They need firmness, because love cares and restrictions provide security. They need to be directed away from bad habits toward good ones. When it is necessary, children need to be told *no* because they do not know what is best for them. They need to be allowed to contribute, to feel they are a necessary part of the family unit, and to be shown that they are contributors to and, in some ways, completers of your happiness.

Children need to recognize sin for what it is—willful disobedience—and be taught to distinguish between it and mistakes. They need to be reassured and comforted in their fears, whether real or imagined. They need to learn how to distinguish between fantasy and reality. They need evaluation and praise—honest feedback and deserved compliments.

Children are inveterate information seekers because there

is so much they don't know. Don't mistake their questioning for disrespect or their enthusiasm in exploring for overactivity. They need room to grow, to expand the perimeters and boundaries of their lives, and to be granted independence as they mature. They need a self-identity—to be able to say "This is me and this is what I like about myself." And children need to have fun—to enjoy and savor their youth, rather than being pushed too rapidly toward adulthood.

Children need a godly example, because they learn more from what they see than what they are told. They need to know you always keep your word, unless emergency circumstances drastically alter a situation. They need to see you fail, so they can learn how to handle failure. They need to see you angry, so they can learn how to handle anger. They need to hear you apologize when you make a mistake or cause hurt feelings, so they can learn to forgive and to say "I'm sorry." And they need a home with an open door, where their friends are welcome and there's always room for one more.

Hospitality: An Open Door Policy

Your open door is a ministry of hospitality to your child's friends. Why not encourage your children to bring their friends home? Sometimes this may seem an imposition or an expense (teenagers love to eat!) or an infrigement on privacy, but the advantages of an open door policy are great: When the "gang" is under your roof, you are in control of what they do. Your presence automatically precludes many troublesome situations.

The best way to control peer group relationships, especially during the teen years, is to use your home as the control center for your child's social activities. Recent studies prove that teens who are expected to maintain close family ties and who have quality parental supervision become better adjusted adults. Those who are required to be responsible to and contribute to the family unit and to go places with their families rather than running around with friends make better grades, do not as readily experiment with drugs and sex, and have fewer divorces when they marry.

Ministry To Others

Our home ministries shouldn't be limited to our family members and children's friends; it should extend outward to include a ministry of hospitality to adult neighbors, friends, acquaintances, and even to strangers. Priscilla is truly our model for loving and entertaining strangers, but even before her time, the Lord laid down the ground rule for hospitality. Though given to the Israelites, we can still apply it to our lives today. "When a stranger resides with you in your land, you shall do him no wrong. The stranger who resides with you shall be to you as the native among you, and you shall love him as yourself" (Lev. 19:33–34). Hospitality, by God's definition, is making anyone who enters your home feel welcome, accepted, and comfortable.

It is making them feel at home, like one of the family, rather than like an outsider. I'm reminded of the needlepoint George's aunt Sylvia has in her house, which she certainly lives up to in superlatives.

Friend, you are welcome here,
Be at your ease.
Come when you're ready,
Go home when you please.
We're happy to share with you
Such as we've got;
The bread in the oven,
The soup in the pot.

You don't have to please us
Or laugh at our jokes.
Sit deep and come often,
You're one of the folks.

(Anonymous)

That's true hospitality.

Christ amplified the meaning of the concept when He taught about humility. "When you give a luncheon or dinner, do not invite your friends or your brothers or your relatives or rich neighbors, lest they also invite you in return and repayment come to you. But when you give a reception, invite the poor, the crippled, the lame, the blind, and you will be blessed, since they do not have the means to repay you" (Luke 14:12–14).

Hospitality is a home ministry to the needy and is based on giving without expecting anything in return. It involves true servanthood, which is what Priscilla displayed in opening her home to feed and house others and in providing a place of worship for fellow believers. Practicing true hospitality—providing room and meals and a place of rest for the weary and needy—is a witness of our love for the Lord, both to other Christians and to unbelievers. The apostle John complimented Gaius for being faithful in helping his fellow believers, even those who were strangers. Then he said, "They bear witness to your love before the church; and you will do well to send them on their way in a manner worthy of God" (3 John 6). Hospitality is a reflection of our faith. It is not only opening our homes and hearts to strangers but properly sending them on their way when they leave, even giving them food, clothing, or money to take with them if they are in need.

I realize it isn't easy to welcome strangers into your home, especially today when there is so little reason to trust anyone you don't know; but God's command still stands. Certainly, you should consider your family's personal needs and plan with them whom to invite and when. Privacy and family togetherness are important, but so is hospitality. The writer of Hebrews urged, "Let the love of the brethren continue. Do not neglect to show hospitality to strangers, for by this some have entertained angels without knowing it" (13:1–2). Think of the honor and blessing Priscilla would have missed if she and Aquila had not taken in a stranger named Paul.

We can expand our "other" ministries if we pray for God to give us a concern for those who are lost. We who belong to the Lord often forget what life was like without Him. At times we may even become smug about our Christianity. And those of us whose families are Christian don't carry the horrendous burden of concern for the salvation of loved ones. But that doesn't mean we can be insensitive and apathetic toward those who do not know the Lord. We need to ask Christ to remind us of what it was like to live without Him and to burden us for people living on the brink of a Christless eternity.

You never know how God will bless your ministry of hospitality as you pull others toward Him through the open doors of your home. You never know what joy and peace and satisfaction will come from your various home ministries until you step out in faith and make a fresh, new beginning. You haven't lived until you've had to start over.

Into the World!

Using our homes as the base of operation for our life ministry doesn't mean we should cloister ourselves behind its doors. One of the most stimulating, invigorating ways to minister is to step out in faith into that hostile environment called the world. Yes, our homes are our havens of rest, and because the church is the family of God, it is also a comfortable, secure place, but if we are serious about reaching lost souls and living our lives as ministries, we must not expect the world to beat a path to our doors. Instead we must accept Christ's challenge to go into the world.

One day my husband, who is an aerospace engineer, and I were discussing why people are more afraid of flying than of riding in cars. He responded, "Because flying puts you into a hostile environment." He went on to explain that flying is unnatural for human beings. (Maybe there is some validity to the old theory that if God had wanted us to fly He'd have given us wings.) It takes us away from our normal life support systems and places us totally at the mercy of human judgment and machine. In an airplane we have absolutely no control over what happens to us. Such vulnerability frightens many people. Anyone who flies does so by an act of faith, trusting in an artificial, man-made environment, a machine and the expertise of fallible, human pilots.

Similarly, the world is a hostile environment to a Christian. If we enter it, we, as children of God, are thrown together with children of Satan; we are light and truth set in the total darkness of sin and falsity. Our citizenship is in heaven but we are, for a while, pulled toward that which is earthly. We must walk by faith, just as people fly by faith, and we must trust God to protect us from the evil one and rely on the Holy Spirit to guide us so we can walk about in a hostile environment without fear.

Work for Christ

Your place of employment may be a hostile, worldly environment, but you can view your job or career as a new vehicle by which you can take Christ and His reconciliation into an unbelieving world. Most workers have to be silent witnesses, because most employers don't allow any kind of religious activity at their place of business, and being an effective, on-the-job witness includes maintaining an exemplary employer-employee relationship. Scripture says Christian employees are supposed to obey their employers, be sincere toward them and their work, and be respectful to their superiors, even if they are unreasonable. Both Paul and Peter told slaves to respect and obey their masters at all times (Col. 3:22; 1 Peter 2:18).

Christ is also reflected through our efficiency. A job well done is a ministry in itself. Good help is hard to find, so an employee's sincere effort is a strong witness. You should do all that is required in the best possible way, in the shortest time possible, without complaining. Actually, you should be willing to go beyond what is expected of you, to walk the extra mile of which Christ spoke, and to volunteer help when it is needed. Because many people try to fulfill only minimum requirements on a job, efficient performance will definitely be noted. "Whatever you do, do your work heartily, as for the Lord rather than for men" (Col. 3:23). Remember, ultimately you aren't working for your boss or a company, but for Jesus Christ.

You can also silently minister on the job by enlightening through example. If you behave as a Christian should, people will notice that you are different and sometime, in some way, the Lord will open an opportunity for you to verbally witness to those whose hearts He's prepared. We must also be willing to speak up for what we know is right. When right and wrong, honesty and dishonesty, the honorable and dishonorable clash in the marketplace, we have to maintain our Christian standards, even if doing so threatens our job. In their book, *Christian Women at Work*, Patricia Ward and Martha Stout observe, "Despite such conflicts, the general thrust of Scripture is that we are not to capitulate to the values of the nonbelieving world, but to present an alternative way of living" (p. 47).

I remember a woman who once came to me for counsel. She had discovered that her immediate supervisor was frequently embezzling money from the petty cash fund, and she wondered what I thought she should do. I suggested she tell him she knew about the thievery and ask him to admit it to his boss and try to make amends. The next day she phoned, in tears. Her supervisor had ordered her to keep her mouth shut, promised he would not take any more money, and threatened that if she told anyone he would accuse her of the crime. She knew she had to report the entire thing to her supervisor's boss, but needed reassurance because she was certain the man would carry out his threat.

The following day she reported the embezzlement, and her supervisor did exactly as he had threatened. He claimed she was the guilty party and insisted that she be fired and turned over to the police. But his ploy didn't work. As it turned out, he had been under suspicion for several months, but until that incident the evidence to accuse him was lacking. He was the one who ended up without a job and was charged with grand larceny. When the head of the company asked the woman how she summoned up the courage to report the man, she told him, "I'm a Christian and I felt it was my responsibility before God," to which he replied, "Well, I'd like to meet your God someday because He certainly has a fine woman on His side." She definitely witnessed, or enlightened, by example.

On the job, as well as anywhere, we can edify those with whom we associate. We can build up and undergird our co-workers. We should not be business associates only, but friends as well. Listen to their problems, offer assistance whenever possible, be sensitive to their need for Christ. Preach the gospel by living it.

Have Non-Christian Friends

How can we reach into the world if we only associate with Christians who behave and believe exactly as we do? We can't; so we must cultivate friendships with unbelievers as well as with those of like faith. One of my non-Christian friends is the editor of a soap opera magazine. I did some articles for her and since then she has actively cultivated my friendship by inviting me to lunch and calling me to talk about her problems—and she has a drove of them. She knows exactly what I believe. In one of our earliest conversations she informed me that she was a spirit-medium. After almost choking on my tea, I casually told her that I was also controlled by a Spirit—the Holy Spirit. That started a lively conversation.

She is a lonely, desperate person. Although she knows hundreds of celebrities, she has no one to whom she feels particularly close. Recently, when she phoned with a tale of woe about the two men she was living with intermittently, I told her that her problem wasn't the men but her morality—or lack of it. From Scripture I shared what she needed to do to put her life in order. She listened without disagreeing with me. She hasn't acted on anything yet, but at least she has heard the truth from the Word of God. I know the Lord brought us together and is using me in her life to pull her toward Him. Whether or not she responds is between her and the Lord.

Fellowship with believers is sweet. But to win souls to Christ, a Christian has to be with the lost and establish a witness through example. That's what Christ did.

Circulate Secularly

Some Christians think their giftedness should be confined to ministering in the local church. On the contrary, the world needs to be "salted" with Christ's perspective, and belonging to a secular organization provides a perfect platform from which to speak. In every service we perform, from being a Girl Scout leader to working in the snack bar at the little league field, we take the Lord with us. Jesus called the world a field that is white, ready for harvest, but to reap the crop we have to be where it's growing.

I have a friend who is extremely active on the parent advisory council at a local junior high school. She doesn't stand up in meetings and quote Scripture or criticize ideas others share that run cross-grain to her Christian beliefs, but she incorporates Christian principles into her performance on the committee and exerts a great deal of godly influence. Recently, she was able to thwart a guest lecture by an astrologer who had been invited to an eighth-grade science class to explain the signs of the zodiac and plot astrological charts for the students. She didn't openly bring Christianity into the discussion, but objected on the grounds that such an activity has no place in a science class and that it could be interpreted as a religious activity. Her efforts prevented a satanic force from being exerted on the impressionable minds of junior-high students.

Be Informed

If we want to have an impact on an unbelieving world, we need to keep informed on current secular trends and stay up-to-date on political and social issues. Too often Christians argue from emotion or ignorance or on the grounds that "the Bible says." What the Bible says doesn't matter to someone who doesn't believe in it. To an unbeliever, the *Wall Street Journal* or *Psychology Today* are just as valid as Scripture. I saw this kind of situation repeatedly in relation to the Equal Rights Amendment. Whenever this issue would be mentioned among Christian women, I would ask if any of them had read the amendment itself. The vast majority of these women, I'd say at least ninety percent, had never read the document. My next question was "How can you be for or against something you've never read or personally investigated?"

If I, as a Christian, am going to stand for a specific cause and set forth a plausible case, I need to be informed. I need to do my research and not accept second-hand information on vital issues. Unbelievers will listen better and respect our opinions more if we know what we're talking about and educate ourselves about all sides of an issue.

The exciting truth is that a Christian's life should be a ministry. We have been chosen and called to go into the world. We are ambassadors, ministers of reconciliation. There is no time like the present to step out in faith and expand the scope of your Christian influence and start making your life into a ministry. Follow in Priscilla's footsteps. Try experimenting with some of these suggestions and guidelines and explore new avenues of service.

EIGHT

The Titus Two Technique

"Older women likewise are to be reverent in their behavior, not malicious gossips, nor enslaved to much wine, teaching what is good, that they may encourage the young women to love their husbands, to love their children, to be sensible, pure, workers at home, kind, being subject to their own husbands, that the word of God may not be dishonored"

TITUS 2:3–5.

Christian women today are not much different from the women who lived in New Testament times. Once God reveals Himself to us and we understand and grasp His truth, we testify, as did the woman at the well. Once the Lord touches our hearts with His love and compassion, we want to minister to Him, as did the women who followed Him to the foot of the cross and eventually into the empty tomb. We want to give of

146

our time and substance, as Joanna and many other women did. Moved by love, we seek to serve Jesus Christ, as did Mary, Martha, Mary Magdalene, and hundreds of other women whose lives were regenerated and changed by His presence. And, like Phoebe, Dorcas, and Priscilla, we both need and want to ally ourselves with the fellowship of believers commonly known as the church. Belonging and participating in a church offers a unified witness to an unbelieving world that we are part of the family of God through faith in Christ. Church membership identifies us as Christians and provides a setting for worship, training, growth, and fellowship.

A church ministry is another important and necessary component or sphere of a life ministry. It is probably the one Christians most take for granted because it is the most obvious. Consequently, it may be the one that needs the most evaluation and restructuring. Many times people are misplaced in their church ministries because they haven't carefully thought through how God wants them to use their giftedness and they don't follow their Spirit-planted desires. Within the body of believers there are numerous ways for a woman with the gift of administration to use her talents. If she's a trained musician, she might direct the choir or organize and produce musicals. If she's good at shuffling paper and organizing materials, she might serve as church librarian or set up records or files. If she's able to mobilize and lead people, she might be a Sunday school superintendent or chair a committee.

Obstacles to Finding Our Places

Too often, we take whatever position we're offered, serve wherever we're asked, instead of intelligently deciding where God wants us to be and what He wants us to do. For example, although I am a trained elementary school teacher, I know the Lord does not want me to teach children. He has ordained that my basic teaching ministry be with adults, particularly with women. If I were to accept the position of second grade Sunday school class teacher, I would not be doing God's perfect will, even though I'd be serving the Lord and using my spiritual gift of teaching. If I were to end up where I didn't belong, I would displace the person who should be where I am, pushing the entire body out of alignment.

Sometimes our decisions are affected by the opinions of others, by peer pressure. Sometimes we accept positions or take on jobs because we want to please someone or because we feel guilty and "unspiritual" when we say *no*. Sometimes we're flattered at being asked to serve in a certain position or by people recognizing our abilities and wanting our help. It's easy to agree to do something when someone convinces me that I am the best, or, worse yet, the *only* person for the job. Believing ourselves indispensable is the height of conceit.

Sometimes well-meaning friends pressure us into believing they know better than we what is best for us. We listen to them rather than the silent, inner voice of the Lord, and, as a result, we are misguided. I realize that at times the Lord uses other Christians, especially those closest to us, to confirm decisions and reveal His will, but if there is a conflict between external influences and the subjective, internal leading of the Spirit, we must listen to God. When we say *yes* for any reason other than as a response to the nudging of the Spirit and the dictates of our conscience, we get misplaced.

We also get misplaced because we don't explore the myriad of new and exciting possibilities that are open to us. We get caught between those two famous, overused excuses: "We've always done it this way," and "We've never done this before." Consequently, sometimes we are dissatisfied with what we're doing or we become stagnant. We set up programs rather than ministering to people and end up serving the institution rather than the Lord it represents.

Who Defines Our Ministries?

Many women accept their church's dogma as their own and mold their ministries to it; they make church doctrine the formative factor in their ministries without ever investigating other views and without searching and studying the Scriptures on their own to confirm the validity of those beliefs. The institutionalized church is helpful, necessary, and a source of blessing and fellowship, but sometimes, instead of encouraging and enabling women, it stifles our capacity to minister, limits our opportunities to take risks and try new things, and deters us from moving in faith into new areas of service.

The inherent problem with using the doctrines of the local church as a basis for theology of ministry is that every congregation, even within the same denomination, has differing tenets and interpretations of Scripture. In some ways that's good because it means the local church is structuring itself to meet the individual needs of the people in its congregation. But, in other ways, it is confusing and debilitating. It is a problem I struggled with for years. Many times what the Holy Spirit was leading me to do, and sometimes secretly and supernaturally set up for me to do, was contradictory to what my church viewed as an acceptable ministry for a woman. I'm not talking about differences of opinion over major doctrines, such as the deity of Christ or the inerrancy of Scripture, but about the more debatable interpretations of the place and performance of women within the body of Christ.

For example, at one time I belonged to a church that believed women should never teach men. Period. No exceptions. Yet, when I was invited to do a teacher-training seminar at another fundamentalist church, the majority of the audience was men, including several elders. Later, one of my publishers arranged for me to speak at a pastor's conference. I was convinced that God had opened those opportunities for me. The pastors and committee members who invited me had prayed, seeking God's direction about whom to ask. Those who attended, including many clergymen, learned from me, but my local church later took me to task for overstepping my role as a woman and teaching men.

I didn't want to disobey my church. I do not want to teach men if Scripture truly prohibits it. I don't want to serve as a deacon or elder or be ordained, if God has set those areas off limits to me because I am a woman. Yet, when I turned to the church for answers to my questions, I received conflicting counsel, and all of it from godly men and women who love the Lord, who want His will, who believe that the Bible is the inspired, inerrant Word of God, and who use it as a basis for their conclusions.

One group believes there are no restrictions on the ways women can minister; another draws a line at the ordination and pulpit-position of pastor; another adds that a woman cannot hold the position of elder, and still another eliminates female deacons. Some say women can never teach men or speak in the open assembly; others say they can, but only in areas of practical expertise and not in doctrine. Still others restrict females to teaching only each other and children. Each group validates its views with biblical "proof." Each believes it is right. I have, at times, wept, begging God to show me how to make the wise and correct decision in the light of such conflicting opinion.

The answer the Lord gave me was simple, direct, and from His Word: "Follow me." Follow the opportunities *I* provide for you. Walk the path *I* prepare.

Now, when I am faced with a theological question that affects my performance and ministry, I ask myself one question: What would Jesus want me to do? I now know that no ministry can be defined or determined by the local church. Nor can another Christian, no matter how sincere or how close to me, decide what my ministry should be. I am responsible and accountable to God to follow *His* leading.

This much I have learned from studying the Gospels: Jesus liked, accepted, and validated women. He never shut them out or pushed them away. He appreciated their service, their competency, and their ability to learn and perform. Too often, too readily churches today concentrate on isolated passages about women rather than looking at the example the Lord set, both by word and deed, when He walked the earth in that mysterious God/man form. It is my personal belief that all doctrines concerning women, which are generally interpreted and taught by men, must be examined in relation to the actions, attitudes, and teachings of Christ. We must focus on the Gospels to properly absorb the intent and content of the Epistles. Such an approach eliminates many of the misunderstandings and conflicts about ways women may minister. The Son truly can set us free; free to establish our own, personal theologies of ministry.

Developing Your Own Theology of Ministry

"So then, my beloved . . . work out your salvation with fear and trembling; for it is God who is at work in you, both to will and to work for *His* good pleasure" (Phil. 2:12–13). Each of us, male or female, is charged and obligated to discover God's will for us as individuals, to work out our own life ministry. Let me pass on some simple steps that helped me develop my own theology of church ministry.

Examine the Past

To develop a theology of church ministry, we first need to discover how our present theology developed. Those who came to Christ when they were adults, may have heard only one doctrinal view—the interpretation presented in the church they have been in ever since. That was the case with my husband. He had not attended church as a child and, as impossible as it seems, no one had ever told him about the claims of Christ (including his carnal Christian wife) until he was in his thirties. Naturally, when he accepted the Lord, he also accepted without qualification the doctrines that were taught in our church, which included some that were quite restrictive toward women. Yet, as the years passed, he had to question those views because he saw what God was doing in our lives. As he studied on his own, his views expanded.

I came from a denomination that ordained women and gave them leadership and teaching positions. As a child, I was accustomed to seeing women do the same things in ministry as men. So, I suffered from a sort of "spiritual culture shock" when, after straying for many years, I came back to the Lord and became involved in a church that confined the role of women. Until that time, I'd never realized a person's sex could become a religious issue. Faced with conflicting views of truth, I knew I had to develop my own theology of ministry. Was what I had been previously taught wrong, or was the second interpretation in error? Had my parents, who were wonderful, dedicated Christians, who loved the Lord with all their hearts, been so terribly mistaken? I knew I had to look at where I'd been before I could decide where I was going.

Examine the Present

After sorting through the past, I sorted out my personal beliefs from my past and present beliefs. I listed everything I had been told and taught in the past. Next to those basic beliefs, I listed the ones that now were being presented in my new church. Then I recorded what I personally believed and compared the lists. Part of my confusion subsided when I realized that all of the lists contained basic truths, such as the Virgin Birth, the deity of Christ, participation in the sacraments, the visible and bodily resurrection of Christ, and the imminent Second Coming. God was showing me that certain dogmas must be present in any church in which I participate.

Next, I contrasted the lists. Each of the differences boiled down to a matter of interpretation of Scripture. As a final step, I wrote down my present, basic beliefs about ministry, based on my understanding of God's Word, weighed in the light of His leading in my life. For example, the Bible teaches that God never leads anyone to sin, so if the Holy Spirit leads me, without any manipulation or planning on my part, to teach a group of pastors at a conference, then teaching men cannot be a sin, at least not for me. Examining the present helped me decide what I believed and separate my ideas from those that had been ingrained into my thinking processes by the church, my parents, and Christian teachers.

Examine Your Motives

A third step in developing a theology of ministry is examining your motives. *Why* do you believe as you do? I truly had to search my heart as I worked through major doctrines about a woman's place and role in the body. I had to make sure I wasn't twisting the truth or taking a particular stand so I could do what I personally wanted to do. I had to make certain that I was listening to God and not to myself. I had to be sure that I didn't want to write books just to get my ideas published or to teach seminars just to make a name for myself. I had to reach the point where I honestly told the Lord that if He wanted me to sit in a church with my head covered and pray silently, I would accept that.

As I was weeding through my motives, the Lord recalled to

me His post-resurrection encounter with Peter at the Sea of Tiberias. Three times Jesus asked His beloved disciple, "Do you love Me?" Peter's automatic and zealous response was, "Yes, Lord." But almost as if He didn't believe Peter, Jesus kept asking the question. I had often wondered why, but this day I realized that the Lord was reinforcing the fact that love for the Lord had to be Peter's basic motivation for ministry— for tending Christ's lambs and shepherding and tending His sheep. Jesus ended the conversation by saying "Follow Me" (John 21:19).

Examining my motives helped me see how many things I had been doing to please myself or other people and how lacking I was in love for the Lord. Once my love for Christ became the overwhelming motivational factor in my ministry, I experienced a freedom of spirit like none I had ever known, and it has increased through the years. When I stopped trying to satisfy the demands of the church and started responding to Jesus, my life took on an entirely new meaning.

Examine Other Views

To develop a personal theology of ministry, you need to study various theological views. You will find more than one set of valid beliefs. A good example of contradictory interpretation, which every woman should examine, concerns the office of deacon. The controversy stems from a passage that describes the attributes of a deacon and centers on the verse, "Women must likewise be dignified, not malicious gossips, but temperate, faithful in all things" (1 Tim. 3:11). That sounds simple enough, but it is nestled between two other verses that refer to the office of deacon. The location of the verse about women right in the middle of a passage about deacons has been the source of many theological debates.

Since some churches do not allow women to hold any

church offices, they interpret the word "women" in that passage to mean deacon's wives. Although they allow women in the congregation to perform the same duties as deacons, they do not afford them the title or position of office. Within that mentality, some churches believe that if a man is called to hold the office of deacon, his wife must meet the behavior requirements listed in 1 Timothy 3:11. Some say it means that a deacon must be married; others say it means that if a man becomes a deacon, his wife automatically becomes one too, and that they are called as a team into a service ministry. Many fundamentalist churches refer to women as deaconesses rather than deacons, drawing a distinct separation between male and female service ministries. Some churches interpret the passage as meaning that both men and women can hold the office of deacon and formally ordain them to the position. Such a short, simple verse to cause so much confusion! The only way to make a rational, honest decision is to look at all sides of an issue then draw your own conclusions. Exploring different beliefs will help you make thoughtful, intelligent decisions and create a greater understanding and respect for the opinions of other Christians who believe differently from you.

Examine Your Church

As a fifth step in establishing a personal theology of ministry, take a close, prayerful look at the beliefs of your local church. Do you disagree with them about major issues, or do you feel your ministry is being subdued or thwarted? If so, you should relocate to a church that more closely supports your beliefs. Don't stay, expecting the church to change to suit you. And don't expect to agree one hundred percent with all of the doctrines of any church. That isn't possible. The most learned scholars hold divergent opinions about many tenets of the faith. But do look for a place where you can worship and serve in the freedom of the Spirit and following the dictates of your heart.

George and I have found a church that wants full participation of women in ministry, that uses their gifts of leadership, prophecy, and teaching as readily as helps and mercy. That's where we're most comfortable and can serve most effectively.

Examine Scripture

A final, but extremely important step in developing your own theology of ministry is to examine Scripture, especially Christ's life and His approach to women and their service. Familiarize yourself with all the passages about women in the Old and New Testaments. Study the lives of women in the Bible. Studying about Priscilla helped me develop a basic principle about women in ministry.

Examining the Scripture puts us in touch with the teaching and leading of the Holy Spirit, who, incidentally, is the Author of the Text we're supposed to follow. Part of my confusion resulted from being "overtaught": I'd received so much conflicting information, all of it from reliable sources, that I wasn't able to decipher it. One day as I was reading the Bible, God gave me this verse. "As for you, the anointing which you received from Him abides in you, and you have no need for anyone to teach you; but as His anointing teaches you about all things, and is true and is not a lie, and just as it has taught you, you abide in Him" (1 John 2:27). God was telling me that *I* am responsible to learn the truth for myself; that my primary teacher and resource for interpretation must be the Holy Spirit. Tapes and books, commentaries, sermons, and Bible lessons are all sources for gaining knowledge, but they take a second place to God's personal instruction through His Spirit. That kind of instruction comes only when I open the Book and study on my own initiative. Relying on secondary sources can be detrimental to developing a personal theology of ministry, because you are giving someone else permission to tell you what you should believe. Now, when I'm faced with a dilemma and have to decide what stand to take on a particular doctrine, the first thing I do is turn the pages of Scripture. I search out God's truth first, in a one-on-one class that is conducted by my Guide and Counselor, the Holy Spirit.

For some reason, many Christian women are willing to let men—their pastors, husbands, or Bible teachers—interpret Scripture for them. They rely on a "middleman," and as a result have not become personal students of the Word. In *Woman Be Free*, Pat Gundry observed that, "Perhaps part of the reason women are so restricted in our churches is that there has been almost no feminine perspective in either Bible translation or interpretation for over 1800 years. Different people see different facets of truth. If the experiences of half of Christendom are not applicable to the careful study and translation of the Scriptures, then we are bound to miss a great deal and perhaps make mistakes a wider experience would prevent" (pp. 2, 11).

We must learn for ourselves, as God intended us to. He does not mean for any other person to study for me or tell me what to believe. Through His written Word, He means to communicate Himself to me as an individual.

The Titus Two Technique

Once you become a student of the Word and start establishing a personal theology of ministry, you'll be better equipped to serve in your local body. Although a Titus Two ministry is only one of many avenues of church-related service open to women, it is a vital one and a good place to make a new beginning, because it is so clearly outlined in Scripture.

The true church isn't a place, it's people. It isn't a building, it's the family of God. The saints who founded the church weren't concerned with where the congregation met or with the formal structure of the body but with who the church was. When the apostle Paul instructed Titus how to set matters in order in the church at Crete, he didn't tell him how to find a nice meeting place, establish committees, or set up programs. He dealt with three major concerns: the behavior of believers, the content of the teaching, and the general responsibilities of specific groups within the church, such as leaders, younger and older men, younger and older women, servants and masters, and members in general.

Within his epistle to Titus, Paul set forth one specific responsibility for Christian women to fulfill as part of their church ministry: Older women are responsible for teaching the younger. This special charge is not restrictive. It certainly doesn't describe the only things women can or should do in the church, nor does it mean young women can't teach. Paul simply lays down one framework upon which the church should be built. Let's look further into this Scriptural technique as an avenue for our church ministries.

Qualifications for Service

Paul stated two basic qualifications for those who participate in this Titus Two church ministry. They must be older women and must live exemplary, godly lives. The word older means *aged*. This is a woman-to-woman ministry where women who are older in years, who are more experienced in life, who have learned many valuable lessons as they have walked with the Master, nurture young Christian women toward spiritual maturity.

These younger women are not responsible to teach themselves or to seek out older women, but those who are mature

in the faith are told to reach out to their younger counterparts. Paul did not tell Titus to teach the young women; he
assigned the job to the older women. It is not the pastor's
duty to educate, edify, and encourage the young women in
the church. Don Williams, in his book *The Apostle Paul and
Women in the Church*, says, "Older women have a divine
calling to teach younger women. Younger women will learn
the practical Christian life not from Titus but from older wom-
en. That life must be demonstrated to be understood. The
training of younger women is designed to support a Christian
home that will be exemplary. . . . The motive in all this
teaching is to honor the word of God" (p. 127).

This approach does not exclude any woman because of age.
All women are included, because someone is always younger
than any of us. It is an overlapping service in which women of
all ages can use their gifts to teach, train, and build up one
another. Also, an older woman can be one who has more
experience and expertise in a given area, so service is not
restricted or limited solely because of a person's chronological
age.

Here is one example of how the Titus Two Technique
might work: Junior-high girls could be trained to work as
teacher's aides in the Sunday school, thus ministering to preschool and elementary-age children. Senior-high girls could
be assigned as big sisters to junior-high girls, and college girls
could become big sisters to high-schoolers. Career women
could counsel high-school and college students about finding
jobs, employer-employee relationships, and witnessing in the
marketplace. Young mothers could give baby-sitting courses
to junior-high and high-school girls. Mothers could advise
expectant mothers. Women with children in the elementary
grades could teach mothers of preschoolers, toddlers, and
infants how to parent. Mothers of teenagers could do the
same for mothers of preteens. Older women could disciple

younger ones in the homemaking arts and time management. Grandmothers could provide wise counsel for women whose children are leaving home, or they might take part in a grand-mother-grandchild program, for young families whose children have no grandparents. The possibilities are limitless! The continuity, sense of community, and bonding and enrich-ment of lives that spring from this type of ministry are invalu-able. And, although all females in the church will be affected and blessed by the ministry, it is up to the older women to initiate and implement it.

Before Paul outlined the general content of a Titus Two ministry, he set down behavior standards for the participants. "Older women . . . are to be reverent in their behavior, not malicious gossips, nor enslaved to much wine, teaching what is good" (Titus 2:3). I interpret Paul's injunction to mean that ministering women are to be temperate and modest. Modesty is another old-fashioned word, like dignity and delight, that has been displaced by the flagrant, excessive behavior of re-cent generations. Modesty means *freedom from excess; being restrained by a sense of propriety.*

A Titus Two woman is modest in action and attitude, rever-ent in behavior. She is a woman who fears the Lord and whose behavior reflects her awe and adoration for Him. Her modesty shows in the way she acts. She is respectful, courte-ous, and thoughtful and possesses "the imperishable quality of a gentle and quiet spirit, which is precious in the sight of God" (1 Peter 3:4). She has a peaceful spirit and isn't easily agitated because she knows God is in control. She keeps her composure because she is rooted in faith and grounded in the love of Christ.

Her modesty shows in the way she talks; she does not gossip or talk unbecomingly about others, spread rumors, betray confidences or speak harshly or thoughtlessly. She doesn't talk too much because she knows "where there are many words, transgression is unavoidable" (Prov. 10:19). She realizes the power of words, that they can hurt and hinder or enlighten and uplift, so when she speaks "she opens her mouth in wisdom, and the teaching of kindness is on her tongue" (Prov. 31:26).

Her modesty and love for the Lord are reflected in the way she dresses. She isn't preoccupied with externals because she realizes that "Charm is deceitful and beauty is vain" (Prov. 31:30). She follows God's way, which is for "women to adorn themselves with proper clothing, modestly and discreetly" (1 Tim. 2:9). She dresses becomingly, not seductively, or in any way that might distract from her godliness.

Her modesty shows in the way she approaches life. In New Testament times, wine was the most common beverage. Water was often contaminated, as well as scarce, so wine was always served with meals. People often lingered over their after-dinner wine, much like we do over coffee and dessert. It was easy to drink too much, so, as an example of temperate behavior, Paul noted that Christian women were to exercise self-control toward alcohol. In a broader sense, this implies we must practice self-restraint and use moderation in all areas of our lives.

A godly woman isn't an excessive or compulsive person and practices temperance in all matters. Her lifestyle reflects and enhances her Christianity. Unbelievers look at her and say, "That's what it means to be a Christian." She is a role model for other Christian women. They look at her and say, "That's what I'm supposed to be." When they see her, they should see a valid representation of Jesus, and her conduct teaches what is good.

Teachers of Good

Teaching what is good is the foundation of a Titus Two ministry. The older woman is a pacesetter who illuminates the Word of God through both formal instruction and active discipleship. She is a friend, a paraclete like the Holy Spirit, who comes alongside to enlighten, edify, guide, and direct. She is an advisor and mentor who counsels from the Word of God, and, in many ways, she is like a mother who teaches perserverance by her commitment, who encourages and comforts.

This is to be a ministry of encouragement: older women are to teach the younger ones . . . that they may *encourage* them. Those of us who have lived awhile have survived innumerable problems, traumas, and tragedies. Because God has upheld us through severe circumstances, we can offer hope to young women who are facing similar dilemmas. We've learned how to cope and overcome and can pass on the benefit of our experience and expertise.

Young women today face countless discouragements. Distinguishing good from evil is not as easy now as it was in the forties and fifties when many of us grew into adulthood. Choices were then more clear cut. Society itself served as a moral restraint. Smoking and drunkenness were socially unacceptable, and drug abuse was almost unheard of. I wasn't offered drugs until I was in my second year of college; my thirteen-year-old son was given his first chance to use them when he was in third grade.

In the past birth control was "iffy" at best. If a girl had premarital sex and got pregnant, abortion wasn't a viable option. If a girl was sexually promiscuous she knew she might very well end up with a baby and a ruined reputation. That was reason enough to refrain from illicit sexual activity. But today, girls who don't have sex before marriage are considered maladjusted.

Divorce wasn't much of an option either. Legal and social barriers made it exceedingly difficult to end a relationship that was presumed to last until death. People worked harder

at solving problems within their marriages. And older generations haven't lived with the threat of nuclear extinction or the
fear that their babies would be born malformed because of
erroneous prescribing of medication or environmental con-
tamination.

It is much more difficult to raise children now, than it has
been in earlier decades. Rearing our daughters during the
turbulent sixties was much easier than raising Brian, who was
born in 1969. Sin is more overt, evil more pronounced, wick-
edness more bold and blatant, and perversion more accepted
as the norm. Young women need encouragement; they need
to be assured that, although society may have changed, Jesus
Christ is still the same and can meet their every need. They
need to be given the hope that if they establish Christian
homes, love their families, and raise their children according
to the precepts in God's Word, they do not need to fear the
future.

Titus Two Principles

Several principles compose the general content of the Titus
Two ministry and are the basis for what is taught and exemplified by the older women. They are to teach the young
women to love their husbands and children, to be sensible
and pure, to work in their homes, to be kind, and to be
subject to their husbands. (vv. 4–5) The husband-wife and
parent-child relationships are first on the list because marriage and family are most important and so deeply affect every
other area of a woman's life. Also, the law of love is the
supreme commandment that supersedes all others.

Paul didn't say young women need to be taught to be
clever, socially adept, overly-efficient wives, or supermoms,
but that they must learn *how to love their husbands and
children.* We don't usually think of love as something we need

to learn, but we do. Love isn't something we fall into or stumble over and it doesn't come naturally. Ever since Adam and Eve took that fatal, catastrophic bite of the forbidden fruit, man's and woman's natural inclination has been to hate, to defend and exalt self and resist anyone or anything that disturbs their comfort or happiness. Love is a learned response.

Some of us are fortunate to have come from homes where we learned to love by watching our parents love each other and having them lavish their devotion and discipline on us. Many people haven't had that privilege. Today, numerous young women come from broken or abusive homes. They were never shown affection, never properly cared for or nurtured. What little they know about love they've learned on the street, from the television, the movies, their friends, or their friends' families. They have a very warped perspective of love and the damage they've suffered is compounded by their ignorance when they marry and have children.

We know a couple who are suffering through such a situation. The husband was raised by his strict, unemotional, widowed father. In childhood the husband had no feminine influence except school teachers and the girls he dated. The wife was raised in an orphanage, where she had no adequate parental figures. Now, all of their children are having learning and behavioral problems, and the marriage is on the rocks. The father does what a man "should"—works twelve hours a day, comes home, watches TV, yells at the kids when they bother him; or he hangs out at the bowling alley with his friends just to get away from home. He doesn't talk to his wife or children except to issue orders and has no idea how to relate to his family. The mother, who is a Christian, tries to discipline the children, but she's structured her home much like the institution she knew as a child. Both parents care deeply about their children and are concerned for their welfare; each tries to be a good husband or wife but neither can, because neither learned how to love.

Someone has to train people like them. Someone must teach young women how to love God's way.

Two other lifestyle principles included in a Titus Two teaching ministry are *sensibility and purity.* Young people, by nature, are impetuous and foolish. They need to cultivate wisdom and learn how to reason and use common sense. Modern young women have to be taught about the modesty I described earlier and they need to be directed in establishing Christian codes of conduct, which may be contrary to their world. A girl whose mother has been divorced twice and has openly had illicit sexual relations doesn't understand that marriage and sex are sacred gifts from God. A young woman whose father has abused her, whose mother is an alcoholic, who has had to lie to keep from being beaten and steal in order to eat, doesn't have much respect for the truth or know how to apply godly values. Conversion is only the first step in a lifetime of spiritual growth. Godliness comes with training.

Another principle in the Titus Two ministry is teaching young women to be *workers at home.* They need to learn how to administrate and operate their abodes, as well as love and serve the people who share them. They need to be taught the fine, time-honored art of homemaking. This phase of the ministry includes time management, cooking, sewing, cleaning, shopping, and every other area of practical expertise a woman needs to transform a house into a home. In no way does the verse infer that a woman cannot be employed outside of her home. Even in the conservative, male-oriented culture of biblical times, godly women didn't devote themselves exclusively to their families. Deborah, a married woman, was a prophet, judge, and military leader. The Proverbs 31 woman dealt in real estate and ran a boutique in the marketplace, where she sold linen garments and belts, among other items.

As noted before, Priscilla was a tentmaker; Eunice, Timothy's mother, had to earn a living in some way that was pleasing to the Lord. Paul was simply saying that women who have homes should be taught how to be good homemakers.

The older women are also to teach the younger to be *kind*. Every time I see a tired, exasperated young mother dragging her toddler down the aisle of a supermarket, I think of this Titus Two principle. Whenever I hear one angrily yell at her child, I am reminded of it. Whenever I hear a wife verbally belittle her husband or mock him with a critical attitude, the word *kind* comes to mind. Life has been so cruel to so many people that they have never learned what kindness is.

Teaching kindness isn't as simple as holding a class titled "How to Be Kind to Your Husband, Children, and Dog." It involves showing young women how to cope with and manage stress situations that make them lash out, lose their tempers, and drive them to the brink of frustration—how to change their attitudes and control their reactions. It includes teaching the meaning of kindness; kindness is displaying good will rather than ill will, backing off when it would be easier to attack, forgiving instead of holding a grudge, being tender instead of harsh, reaching out in compassion instead of withdrawing in selfishness. Kindness is a loving heart in motion. This means older women will have to perform acts of charity, generosity, and grace for the younger ones and open their homes to the young women.

The final basic principle in a Titus Two ministry relates to the husband-wife relationship. Young women must be helped to understand the *one-flesh relationship*, their husbands' role and function in their lives, and that both the husband and wife must acknowledge and respect each other's God-given position. They need to learn the meaning of marriage and that "being subject to their own husbands" is another way of saying "love does not seek its own" (1 Cor. 13:5).

All of these Titus Two principles are things that only women can capably teach. Men can teach doctrine about such subjects, but a man can't teach a woman how to be a good wife or mother or homemaker. There *is* a difference between the sexes. That's why the Spirit led Paul to make the older women in the church responsible for certain kinds of teaching. There are things about the feminine nature that men cannot translate into practical experience.

Purposes of the Ministry

A Titus Two ministry is an essential ingredient in the body of Christ. Without it, Christian young women are left to their own devices and their spiritual growth is stunted. Also, their lives do not glorify God as they should or could. Paul said the primary purpose for teaching and discipling the church's young women is so that the Word of God will not be maligned or dishonored. We minister so people won't point accusingly at our young women and say, "If that's what a Christian is like, I don't want to be one." Older women who do not fulfill this scriptural charge are, through a sin of omission, partially responsible for bringing shame on the Lord.

There are numerous secondary purposes for a Titus Two, woman-to-woman ministry. It deepens the participants' personal relationship with Jesus Christ and produces satisfactory role models for women. It prepares Christian women for life ministry and undergirds their homes and marriages. It provides much needed support systems, through teaching, prayer groups, and counseling, and is a source of fellowship and friendship. It provides opportunities for women to reproduce their faith in others, to sharpen their skills, to develop leadership ability, to use their giftedness, and it opens avenues of service. It promotes Bible study and helps women grow in grace and knowledge of the Lord Jesus Christ.

Getting the Word Out

A Titus Two ministry is based on actions more than words, on *showing* rather than *telling*. For this kind of discipling to occur, older women have to get to know the younger ones, identify their needs, and offer themselves in friendship. A preacher quoted Charles Spurgeon as saying, "It is not enough to seek or even find lost sheep. They, afterwards, must be tended, led and fed." This can be done informally, on a one-on-one basis. An older woman can take a younger one "under her wing," invite her into her home, incorporate her into her life, and show her how to do things by doing them with her. My friend Jo Kreiger taught me how to study the Bible and prepare lessons by sitting down with me at her kitchen table, week after week, and showing me, step by step, how to outline a passage, do word studies, and develop principles. Sue taught Sandy how to make a household budget and balance her checkbook by doing it with her and explaining each step.

Teaching can also be done in small groups that meet informally in homes or at the church. They may be just for prayer, sharing, and fellowship or they can include Bible study. The large church I attend calls this kind of discipling *enabling*. These groups create smaller church families within the bigger congregation. People are trained as enablers and they minister effectively in this personal, practical way.

Formal Instruction

Any Titus Two ministry should also include formal Bible studies. To walk in a manner befitting God's people, women must be immersed in God's Word. For any effective change in personal behavior or ongoing eternal significance, their souls must be cut with the two-edged sword. Some classes will be formed on the basis of need, such as a "Beloved Un-believer" class for women who are unequally yoked, or classes in parenting for mothers of toddlers, preschoolers, elemen-tary-age children, and teens. Some should be topical studies, based on the various interests of the women in the church; some may be age-graded, but every church should have one churchwide women's Bible study where women of all ages can assemble weekly around the Word. The purpose of these Bible studies is to teach the Word, to teach how to apply and study Scripture, and to help the women use their faith in practical ways.

I know firsthand that these study groups bear remaining fruit. In the early sixties I was privileged to attend one of the first Campus Crusade Action Groups in the Los Angeles area. *The Ten Basic Steps to Christian Maturity* was in rough draft form and the class format experimental. Jo Kreiger led the study. Like babies who were learning to walk, we group members took precarious, wobbly first steps toward becom-ing active, ardent disciples of our Lord.

We studied together, hashed out Scripture, argued theol-ogy, and prepared supplemental study materials as needs arose. We counseled each other and prayed through the prob-lems of troubled marriages, unsaved husbands, straying chil-dren, and our own spiritual deficiencies. We rejoiced over victories and answered prayer; we bore one anothers' bur-dens. We received practical, challenging "on the job" train-ing. When we studied the section on prayer, each of us was required to select a prayer partner, to lead the prayer group, to have prayer daily with our families at home, and to keep a prayer diary. When we covered the section on witnessing, we went out, cold turkey, to shopping malls, parks, and parking lots, and verbally shared our faith with strangers. I remember sharing the Lord with an eighty-eight-year-old man who was sitting at a bus stop. He accepted Christ and God used him to open the door to the convalescent home where he lived. Soon after that, every week a team of us was allowed to go in there and teach a Bible lesson to those precious, needy souls.

When we did the section on studying the Bible, each of us had to prepare and present a lesson based on our personal Bible study. (After that, I never stopped.) It was an exciting time. Lives were changed and ministries established.

A few months ago, over forty of us had a reunion. Almost without exception, each of us is still involved in the ministries God established in our lives through that group, and, in most cases, our service is more far-reaching than any of us dared imagine. God has truly supplied in exceeding abundance beyond anything we could have dreamed up on our own. Many of us not only maintained but expanded our areas of Christian service. The reason is quite simple: We continued to grow and prosper because we had been shown what to do, how to do it, and why, in a Bible study geared to our needs.

Moving Out In Your Church Ministry

I once heard a pastor say, "I doesn't matter if you are educated and motivated unless you're activated." You may be wondering where to go from here, how to activate your church ministry or to start or expand a Titus Two ministry in your church. The following six steps will help you move out in service.

Identify. First, assess what's currently happening in your church. Does it have any sort of Titus Two ministry? They may not be tagged as such, but there are probably many women's activities. Nearly all churches have a missionary organization and a fellowship group. To help you discover what's going on now in your church, list all the women's functions and organizations, then the basic purpose of each class, group, or organization. The list will show what is and isn't being done. You may also want to explore the possibility of serving on a board or committee that serves the church body at large and is not exclusively involved with ministering to women.

Initiate. Next, list any personal ministries you are performing in your church. Decide what you *want* to do, what your church ministry should be. Reevaluate what you are currently doing in the light of your giftedness and Spirit-planted desires. Make a list of areas in which you feel you can, or earnestly want to, serve. Don't make any quick or radical changes until you've set goals and prayed about your decision. And honor any commitments you have before moving on.

Integrate. Find out how and where your desired ministry will fit in to the overall scheme of things in your local church. Work within its governmental framework and go through existing channels. Don't overstep boundaries or sidestep authority. Integrating takes time and patience. Recruiting allies helps. Think of other friends or acquaintances who might be interested in expanding or revamping their ministries, and share your ideas with them.

Infiltrate. When establishing new ministries, try to build on existing programs. A Titus Two ministry should be an extension of existing programs. Ongoing organizations such as circles, Bible studies, and women's missionary groups are serving a purpose and meeting needs, otherwise they wouldn't exist. Try to fit in rather than phasing out. Offer your services to the right people in the right way. Don't try to displace anyone, but create a place for yourself. List some ideas you want to share with your pastor or the leader of your choice in your church. Be ready to explain what you want to do, why you want to do it and what needs it will meet.

Implement. Once you've identified, initiated, integrated, and infiltrated, you're ready to implement. Activate your ministry. Do one new thing or make changes that will add depth and dimension to your present ministry.

Involve. Share your life with at least one other person. Reach out to someone. Offer yourself. If you're an older woman, disciple a young one. If you're a younger woman who needs to be discipled, ask an older woman to be your friend in Christ. Start touching people's hearts by making yourself available to them in your church and your home.

But I'm Afraid

"What if it doesn't work?" you may be asking. "What if I try something new and I fall on my face?" We live in a success-oriented world where failure is looked upon as a cardinal sin. This drive for success has made us production, rather than performance, oriented, and has caused many Christians to center their life ministries around programs instead of people. We are much more concerned about what we accomplish than the manner in which we accomplish it or whom it helps. We are overly concerned about the opinions and reactions of others. We're embarrassed by mistakes and defeated by wrong outcomes. We think we've failed if we try something and it doesn't work or turns out differently than we thought it should or would. Consequently, we avoid taking risks or stepping out in faith on untried ground. We start depending on ourselves, forgetting that our confidence and competency in ministry come from the Lord and are not produced through our own feeble, fallible human efforts. Self-sufficiency and self-confidence give birth to defeat, but Christ-confidence and God-competency assure success, regardless of outcomes.

Fear of failure subsides when we realize that we cannot fail in anything if we totally rely on the Lord. "Such confidence as this is ours through Christ before God. . . . Our competence comes from God. He has made us competent ministers of a new covenant" (2 Cor. 3:4–6). Placing our confidence in Christ and admitting that our competence stems from God rather than from our own intellect, capabilities, or talents, frees us to minister in the Spirit and keeps us from giving up in the face of adversity.

We need to redefine failure. Failure isn't trying and not achieving the desired results; failure is not trying at all. Someone whose name has gotten lost in the annals of literature but who understood human nature said, "Aim for a star! Never be satisfied with a life that is less than the best. Failure lies only in not having tried, in keeping the soul suppressed."

Success isn't achieved through perfect performance but by mastering defeat. Someone once said that success is doing something for the twentieth time and finally getting it right. Failure isn't being knocked down but not getting up when we are. Failure isn't making mistakes but giving up when we do. Failure isn't losing the race, or coming in second or tenth or last place, but refusing to run in the first place. We need to remember that God is more concerned with our motives and our methods than He is with outcomes, which are in His hand anyway.

We must trust God with the outcome of our ministries because we don't have the capability to structure or control circumstances or to know what is best. We are limited by our humanity. We don't do things the way God does them; we don't think as He thinks. "For My thoughts are not your thoughts. Neither are your ways my ways, declares the Lord. 'For as the heavens are higher than the earth, so are My ways higher than your ways and My thoughts than your thoughts'" (Isa. 55:8–9). Serving in obedience and leaving the consequences up to God eliminates failure.

We should trust the results to God because we are shortsighted. We never think or act with the long-term view that He does. When we do things our way we limit God's supernatural outpouring in our lives because He "is able to do exceeding abundantly beyond all that we ask or think" (Eph. 3:20). No matter what our plans or how lofty our goals, God's best for us always surpasses them. We cannot fail if we follow the leading of the Lord and trust God for results.

Another essential in overcoming fear of failure is learning to rest in God's perfect love. The apostle John wrote that "There is no fear in love, but perfect love casts out fear" (1 John 4:18). We usually think of hatred as being the opposite of love, but this verse indicates that fear is its antithesis. Think about it for a moment. We never fear someone who truly loves us because there is *no* fear in love. I am not, never have been, and never will be afraid of my husband. I know he would never purposely do anything to hurt me. Because he loves me, I trust him completely with my life, my emotions, and my innermost thoughts.

We know that the Father loves us with a perfect, unconditional love. We are His beloved. That overwhelming fact should eliminate fear from our lives. Fear enters into a relationship when someone breaks trust. When they've disobeyed or misbehaved, children become afraid of their parents. Disobedience is the open door through which fear enters the God-human relationship. When we sin, we negate trust and are consumed by fear, just as Adam and Eve were when they hid from God in the Garden after they took that fateful bite of the forbidden fruit.

We, who belong to God through Jesus Christ, become fearful when we are not submerging ourselves in the Father's perfect, agape love. We can sing with the psalmist, "The LORD is for me; I will not fear. What can man do to me?" (118:6). Christians have no reason to fear failure or hold back from total commitment to ministry. Each step they take, every event in their lives, each circumstance that crosses their path is ordained by a sovereign, loving, caring God.

A final way to overcome fear of failure is to program for success. Every magazine or newspaper I read contains ads urging people to attend various kinds of "success seminars." One recent ad in the *Los Angeles Times* promised: "In thirty days you'll go from being a nobody to being a somebody who earns a minimum of $50,000 a month." Another claimed: "We'll teach you how to get what you want, when you want it and we'll show you how to use people to get what you want."

God understands that people want and need to succeed; He also wants us to, but He wants our success to be according to His standards. Thousands of years ago the Lord gave His servant, Joshua, a foolproof formula for success that is just as meaningful and applicable today as it was then.

God's formula for success in Joshua 1:7–8 contains five steps. "Only be strong and very courageous; be careful to do according to all the law which Moses My servant commanded you; do not turn from it to the right or to the left, so that you may have success wherever you go. This book of the law shall not depart from your mouth, but you shall meditate on it day and night, so that you may be careful to do according to all that is written in it; for then you will make your way prosperous, and then you will have success."

The first is to *be strong and courageous*. Success involves commitment—refusing to give up, facing criticism, sometimes even ridicule. This takes courage and strength of character. But we don't have to do this on our own. When the Lord commanded Joshua to be strong and courageous He also promised that He would be with him, wherever he went (v. 9).

The second step to success is to *do things God's way*, diligently to follow His moral code and adhere to His standards. The world says it's all right to manipulate, to lie in order to tip the scales in our favor, to toot our own horns, to look out for number one, but those aren't God's methods. If we are going to succeed in our ministries, we cannot take any shortcuts. We have to adhere cautiously to all of God's law, not out of some legalistic duty but as a code of conduct that will bring positive results.

The third step to success is *don't get sidetracked*. The Proverbs warn that we should not turn to the right or left of God's way. It's so easy for us to go our own direction, to take our eyes off Christ and wander from His chosen way for us. The other day I asked Brian to clean out all of the drawers in his desk. They were crammed with a year's accumulation of school papers along with creepy crawlies and all those gunky things boys collect. An hour later, when I went to see how he was doing, one drawer was open, a few papers were scattered on his desktop and he was lying on his bed reading a book of baseball facts he'd found in the drawer. "I forgot I had this!" he explained. Meanwhile, the drawers didn't get cleaned.

We get sidetracked like that. We find something that interests us or stumble over something from the past and step out of God's will. If we want to succeed we have to concentrate on following the Lord and fulfilling our commitment to Him.

The fourth step in the success process is to *meditate on God's Word,* which means more than reading the Bible, studying the Scriptures, or thinking about the Lord. It means keeping His ways, His law, His will for our lives uppermost in our minds, so that through constant usage they become ingrained in our hearts. Meditating on the law literally means being preoccupied with God rather than with self; letting the sweetness of His presence and the beauty of His thoughts permeate our souls. Meditating on the law is tuning in to God.

The final step toward success is carefully to *obey*. As Christ emphasized in the parable of the wise and foolish men, knowing and hearing are not sufficient; we will succeed and prosper only if we consistently and carefully obey.

Making Your Life A Ministry

God has called us to be His people. He has fashioned us, through His wise, sovereign design, into a spiritual, yet corporal Body. He has redeemed us from sin, commanded us to be holy, called us to minister, gifted and empowered us for service, and privileged us to bear His name and do His work. We are His beloved, His children, His Bride, His church. As women with that standing, daughters of the King, we must activate the Priscilla Principle. Every Christian woman must look upon her life as an ongoing ministry to her precious Lord. What you do should be determined by the leading of the Holy Spirit, your giftedness, and the opportunities God sets in your path. You must take personal responsibility for defining God's will and developing a theology of ministry based on a thorough knowledge of the Scriptures. Like Priscilla, you must accept the challenge of your calling and make your life a ministry.

Bibliography

Chafer, Lewis Sperry. *Systematic Theology*. Dallas: Dallas Seminary Press, 1948.

Christie, Jean Marie. "A Nightmare Journey Through Burnout," *Family Life Today*, March 1982.

Cramer, Raymond. *The Psychology of Jesus and Mental Health*. Grand Rapids: Zondervan, 1959.

Deen, Edith. *Wisdom From Women in the Bible*. New York: Harper and Row, 1978.

Dodson, Fitzhugh. "Family Happiness is Homemade," *Family Life Today*. November 1983.

Fee, Gordon, and Douglas Stuart. *How to Read the Bible for All Its Worth*. Grand Rapids: Zondervan, 1982.

Gundry, Patricia. *Woman Be Free*. Grand Rapids: Zondervan, 1977.

Kessler, Jay. *Too Big to Spank*. Ventura: Regal Books, 1978.

Kuyper, Abraham. *Women of the New Testament*. Grand Rapids: Zondervan, 1962.

Stout, Martha, and Patricia Ward. *Christian Women at Work*. Grand Rapids: Zondervan, 1981.

Vine, W. E. *Expository Dictionary of New Testament Words*. Old Tappan: Fleming H. Revell, 1940.

Wald, Oletta. *The Joy of Discovery in Bible Study*. Minneapolis: Augsburg Publishing, 1975.

Williams, Don. *The Apostle Paul and Women in the Church*. Ventura: Regal Books, 1977.